D1617264

What's Your Literacy IQ?

What's Your Literacy IQ?

Test Yourself on Your General Knowledge
and Literacy — 1,200 Questions on
Subjects From Abacus to Zygotes

by
Norma Gleason

A Citadel Press Book
Published by Carol Publishing Group

A Citadel Press Book
Published by Carol Publishing Group
Citadel Press is a registered trademark of Carol
    Communications, Inc.
Editorial Offices: 600 Madison Avenue, New York, N.Y. 10022
Sales & Distribution Offices: 120 Enterprise Avenue, Secaucus,
    N.J. 07094
In Canada: Canadian Manda Group, P.O. Box 920, Station U,
    Toronto, Ontario M8Z 5P9
Queries regarding rights and permissions should be addressed to
    Carol Publishing Group, 600 Madison Avenue, New York, N.Y. 10022

Carol Publishing Group books are available at special discounts
for bulk purchases, for sales promotions, fund raising, or
educational purposes. Special editions can be created to specifications.
For details, contact: Special Sales Department, Carol Publishing
Group, 120 Enterprise Avenue, Secaucus, N.J. 07094

Manufactured in the United States of America
10 9 8 7 6 5 4 3 2 1

Library of Congress Cataloging-in-Publication Data

Gleason, Norma.
    What's your literacy IQ? : test yourself on your literary and
general knowledge : over 1,000 questions on subjects from abacus to
zygotes / by Norma Gleason.
        p.   cm.
    "A Citadel Press book."
    ISBN 0–8065–1389–6
    1. Questions and answers.   I. Title.
AG195.G56   1993
031.02—dc20   92–39178
                                                      CIP
                                                      Rev

Contents

v

To the Reader

First things first: The term *literate*, as used in this book, does not mean being able to read and write, but rather, another definition offered in *Webster's Ninth*: "educated, cultured... having knowledge or competency."

*

It is also necessary to say that this "test" is not a scientific assessment of your intelligence and/or literacy.

The scope of anyone's knowledge cannot be definitively evaluated with 1,050 questions. It would be possible, although unlikely, for a highly literate person to do badly because he doesn't happen to know the answers to the specific questions in this book, although he may know the answers to thousands of other questions that were not asked.

On the other hand, I think it safe to say that in general the reader will get a roughly accurate (forgive the oxymoron) idea of how much he knows.

*

I rejected the usual format of categories such as Art, Literature, Films, and so on in order to use questions on a wider variety of topics. Had I used categories, my work would have been easier. I could, for instance, have looked for 20 questions in each of 51 categories. Instead I selected questions on hundreds of different topics, not just 51, to give the reader a fairer chance to use what he knows.

*

The questions in the first section of this book are divided into 21 alphabetical categories. Answers to questions in the A category must begin with the letter A and so on.

Categories are as follows:

A B C D E F G H I JK L M N O PQ R S T UV WX YZ

In the JK, PQ, UV, WX, and YZ categories the answer may begin with *either* letter.

To get the best possible score, don't forget which letter or letters you are to use as the first letter of your answer.

See Scoring.

Not only do alphabetical categories allow unlimited source material, there is a side benefit as well. Recollection is called up in this book via the letter of the alphabet with which the answer word begins. A reader may know the name of the hound that guards Hades, yet be unable to bring it to mind. The letter C is a memory jog that may provide access to the name.

*

Cautionary note: The reader will see many easy questions in the book. That is deliberate; the easy questions are the basic ingredient with which are mixed questions of greater and greater difficulty. If all were difficult, it would take more than a literate person to answer them; it would take a near genius.

For instance, easier questions are B–3, E–44, and O–35. Of medium difficulty are JK–39, E–23, and E–41. Tough questions (for most) are E–42, M–8, and YZ–45.

*

One final note: Have fun with this book! After all, that is its main purpose—to divert you, entertain you, and challenge you.

Good luck.

Scoring

Use paper and pencil to list your answers for each category. Then turn to the answer section to see how many you got right. Each correct answer counts for one point. Use the following rating chart:

Under 25–not passing

25 to 30–low average

31 to 35–average
36 to 40–high average
41 to 45–superior
Over 45–outstanding

Add your scores for all 21 categories and divide by 21 to get your overall rating.

How Others Did

You might like to check your score against the scores of ten knowledgeable people who were given 50 questions to answer from this book—25 A questions and 25 JK questions.

Lowest score was 20, not quite passing. Highest (hard to top) was 47½.One of the most-missed questions was A–19, the violin-makers.

Participants, expectedly, had more trouble with the JK questions, because this time they had two choices for the initial letter of the answer. JK–18, the Indian tribe, baffled eight of the ten guinea pigs. Many could not correctly answer JK–12, Chinese god or idol, and had difficulty with JK–10, actor in *Semi-Tough*.

Wrong answers or no answers were given by at least one person for almost every question. Some wrong answers: A–10, aphrodisiac; A–5, anthropod; A–14, Stradivarius (doesn't begin with A); A–20, squirrels (again doesn't begin with A); A–24, addition; JK–10, James Cagney (doesn't begin with JK); JK–12, jinn; and JK–13, koala.

There are enough easy questions so that, unless you're having a bad day, you should have no trouble scoring at the basic 25 to 30 mark. Anything over that is icing on the cake.

Acknowledgments

Book projects like this are rarely accomplished without help.

My friend Ann Larberg spent many hours proofreading the manuscript with me, as well as giving support and encouragement along the way. Responsibility for any errors that escaped our scrutiny is mine.

Despite a busy schedule, my daughter, Susan Jones, helped with research, having accesss to larger libraries than I do.

And my friend Virginia Weise helped check the copyedited work by reading the answers aloud so I could compare them with the revised questions.

Members of a book discussion group in Ann Arbor, Michigan were gracious enough to serve as guinea pigs, allowing me to evaluate their responses to 50 of the questions taken from 2 alphabetical categories. This helped me to refine the scoring system.

And I am grateful to the publishers of the many reference books whose indexes I scoured to get ideas for these questions.

Thank you all.

What's Your Literacy IQ?

Section I
Questions

Questions of random selection with alphabetical clues.

A taste of every sort of knowledge
is necessary to form the mind.
John Locke

1. Ingrid Bergman starred in this 1956 movie, playing the part of an amnesia victim who might be the daughter of a Russian czar.

2. Large seabird found around the Cape of Good Hope. Sailors believed that to shoot one would bring them harm.

3. He was tutor to Heloise, a beautiful young girl, and they fell in love.

4. Moorish citadel and palace built at Grenada, Spain, in the 13th century.

5. Sci-fi term for an artificial but humanlike being.

6. Famous photographer who won acclaim for his black-and-white pictures of national parks.

7. Name of Nick and Nora's dog in *The Thin Man* series.

8. The science that deals with the producing of sound and its transmission and effects.

9. Counting device using movable beads strung on wire within a frame.

10. The ancient Greek gods ate this food which made them immortal.

11. Fruit associated with Isaac Newton and the laws of gravity.

12. Phrases such as "babbling brook" and "heavy heart" are examples of _____.

13. Name given by Muslims to their One True God.

14. Another word for the Arabic system of numerals; decimal system of counting.

15. Edible flower head, cooked as a vegetable. When growing, the plant resembles a thistle.

16. King of the Huns, the "Scourge of God."

17. Slang from World Wars I and II meaning antiaircraft guns.

18. Term applied to humans and animals with a congenital lack of color.

19. Violin made by two brothers, Andrea and Nicolò, and their successors, at Cremona. The instrument bears their surname.

20. Cows moo, dogs bark, owls hoot, pigeons coo. What animals gibber?

21. Sailors who voyaged in quest of the Golden Fleece.

22. This tree is also called the "trembling poplar" because it moves with the slightest breeze.

23. Village in Georgia where thousands of Union troops died of their injuries or of illness in a Confederate prison, in part due to terrible conditions.

24. $2x = y = 250$, etc.

25. One of the official languages of South Africa, a mixture of Dutch and other languages.

26. According to legend, this island in the Atlantic Ocean, a site of culture and civilization, became submerged and forever lost.

27. Houseplant of the lily family, with large green leaves often striped with white, used in title of George Orwell novel.

28. Island in San Francisco Bay, for years the site of a federal prison.

29. Artificial sweetener, of which NutraSweet is an example.

30. The bloodstream is filled with thousands of special white cells that attack viruses and bacteria. These cells are called _____.

31. Those who sought to turn base metal into gold during the Middle Ages.

32. Austrian psychiatrist who believed aggression to be the basic human drive.

33. Popular expression meaning experimental, new, unorthodox, in the forefront (originally French).

34. Curly wool from young lambs; a large Russian city.

35. Where Peachtree Street is.

36. Bony-plated rodent found in South America and the southern U.S.

37. Eleventh sign of the Zodiac, Latin for *water-bearer*.

38. Projection of cartilage at the front of the neck (two words).

39. A disease causing loss of appetite and inability to eat, leading to emaciation.

40. Small alcoholic drink taken before a meal to stimulate the appetite.

41. The sounding of the notes of a chord in rapid succession instead of simultaneously.

42. Tennis champion; won at Wimbledon 1975.

43. Wife of our second U.S. President.

44. Secretary of State William Seward bought this land for the U.S. from Russia in 1867 paying over $7 million. It was called Seward's Folly by those who considered it worthless property.

45. Birthstone for the month of February; semiprecious purple or violet stone.

46. Remembered for the courage of Texans who held this fort in San Antonio against a Mexican siege.

47. What aluminum is called in Britain.

48. Mountain in Turkey where Noah's Ark is said to have landed.

49. Chinese medical treatment in which slender metal needles are inserted into the skin at specified points.

50. A high-ranking Muslim religious leader in Iran is given this title.

Score: _____ correct

B

I had six honest serving men—
They taught me all I knew!
Their names were Where and What and When—
And Why and How and Who.

                    Rudyard Kipling

1. Stock-market term for an investor who believes the market will rise and he can sell his shares for a profit.

2. Dutch settlers named this U.S. city after the town of Breuckelen in the Netherlands.

3. Another name for the huge apelike creatures supposedly seen in the U.S. and Canada, also called Sasquatch.

4. This musical instrument is considered to be of Scottish origin, but actually is an ancient instrument once used by the Romans.

5. These animals, the only mammals which can truly fly, have a built-in sonar system based on echoes from their squeaks.

6. General term for a drug that reduces the symptoms of high blood pressure, migraine headaches, and other disorders of the central nervous system, i.e., propranolol (two words).

7. Irish playwright, jailed for his IRA activities. His autobiography is entitled *Borstal Boy*.

8. This hunting knife is named after an American frontiersman who lost his life at the Alamo.

9. Nickname for the predominant theory among astronomers and physicists that the universe began with a stupendous explosion (two words).

10. It used to be East Pakistan; it's in southern Asia and has the highest population density in the world.

11. German composer who wrote the *Moonlight Sonata*.

12. The only dog that cannot bark; an African breed, it whines instead.

13. Gambling game played with cards by a "banker" and players who play against him; originally played in French casinos.

14. In golf, scoring one strike over par on a hole.

15. Derogatory term implying lack of intelligence (slang; two words).

16. French liqueur first made by an order of Roman Catholic monks. It carries their name.

17. A pole with red and white spiral stripes used to stand outside this kind of establishment.

18. Amphibious herbivorous dinosaur, one of the largest known.

19. Frozen dessert formed in a round mold, usually made with ice cream.

20. Fop or dandy, after an English gentleman who set the fashion in men's clothes (two words).

21. Famous painting by Thomas Gainsborough (two words).

22. Name of the character (not the actor) who turned into the Hulk in the TV series.

23. What U.S. fighting men called any large gun or cannon in World War I (two words).

24. Nickname for the doctor on the Starship Enterprise.

25. Gas apparatus used to heat chemical solutions, named after a German chemist (two words).

26. Lively dance step that was popular in the 1920s (two words).

27. This North Dakota city was originally called Edwinton. In 1873 its name was changed to honor the then German Chancellor.

28. Not the clock and not the tower, but the bell that strikes the hour (it's in London; two words).

29. Street in New York City that has become a haven for derelicts.

30. Obsolete little tool once used to fasten shoes or gloves.

31. This American composer wrote "What the World Needs Now Is Love."

32. Meteorological wind scale.

33. Incidents of widespread loss of electric power; temporary loss of consciousness or memory.

34. British term for an attorney who may plead cases in the superior court. A solicitor, also an attorney, may not.

35. The first Prime Minister of Israel; surname.

36. Lennon, McCartney, Harrison, and Starr.

37. What confidence men are jokingly said to try to sell you in New York City (two words).

38. The galago, a small African primate.

39. Term defining the compulsory substitution of different principles or beliefs from those originally held by the subject, achieved through indoctrination and mental torture.

40. The Supreme Court case that barred quota systems in colleges but affirmed the constitutionality of programs giving advantages to minorities (surname of petitioner).

41. In 1789 an uprising took place on this ship. Mutineers cast their commander, Captain Bligh, and others adrift in a longboat.

42. Since 1956 the small island the Statue of Liberty stands on has been called Liberty Island. Its old name was _____.

43. This garment, consisting of loose trousers worn under a short skirt, was invented by a Mrs. Miller, a reformer who wanted to improve women's dress. But the garment was named after another woman who pushed the idea.

44. Greatest epic poem extant in Old English, titled after its hero, who battled monsters and dragons.

45. A system of printing and writing for the blind, named after its French inventor.

46. William F. Cody's nickname.

47. Uninhabited atoll in the Pacific where the atom bomb was first tested in 1946. Its name was borrowed for a skimpy swimsuit.

48. "_____ is willin'." This three-word message to Clara Peggotty through David Copperfield was the message writer's way of proposing marriage to her.

49. In 1930 Cole Porter wrote this song, based on a dance that resembles the rumba.

50. Fortress in Paris, built around 1370 and destroyed during the French Revolution. Its capture on July 14, 1789, is celebrated today as a French national holiday.

Score: _____ correct

C

Learning by study must be won;
'Twas never entailed from sire to son.
John Gay

1. They include cirrus, stratus, and cumulus.

2. Located in New Mexico, these limestone caves are millions of years old and are among the largest in the world (two words).

3. King of old-fashioned slapstick, he played a tramp with baggy pants.

4. The art of beautiful writing.

5. A method of decorating metal objects, such as jewelry, with enamel in various colors.

6. What every decent woman wore in the 1890s.

7. What Marie Antoinette is said to have advised the hungry people to eat instead of bread.

8. Popular resort area in Massachusetts, extending into the Atlantic ocean.

9. Smiling feline in *Alice in Wonderland*.

10. A set of large bells played from a keyboard.

11. Largest living rodent, weighing up to 100 pounds, native to Central and South America.

12. What game can score fifteen two, fifteen four, and a pair is six (six pegs)?

13. Santa has eight reindeer. Their names are Dancer, Vixen, Blitzen, Dasher, Prancer, Donner, _____, and _____ (two words).

14. Venetian author and adventurer whose name became a synonym for seducer. His memoirs became world famous.

15. A noisy feature of yesteryear's circus parade, this musical instrument plays loud, harsh music by means of steam whistles.

16. Emblem of the medical profession.

17. British explorer and navigator who was murdered in the Sandwich Islands (later renamed the Hawaiian Islands).

18. Ornamental ceremonial pipe of the American Indian, also called the peace pipe.

19. Detective in rumpled raincoat played by Peter Falk in TV series.

20. Ten mills in money.

21. What K–9 police aides are.

22. The number represented by a 1 followed by 303 zeroes, or 100 groups of 3 zeroes after 1,000.

23. Lizard found mostly in Africa. Its skin changes color when stimulated by light.

24. Favorite spelling bee word before 1930, when this city was renamed Istanbul.

25. Richard Nixon's dog, a gift from a Texas supporter.

26. Famous American fighting ship, the USS _____, nicknamed Old Ironsides.

27. Muhammad Ali's name before he changed it.

28. Delicacy made from sturgeon's eggs (or other large fish).

29. Where the pilgrims were going to pay respects to the shrine of Thomas à Becket in Chaucer's *Tales*.

30. The three-headed watchdog at the gates of Hades. The possible origin of this myth is the ancient Egyptian custom of guarding graves with dogs.

31. One-eyed giant of mythology. The eye was in the center of the forehead.

32. An unnatural fear of enclosed places.

33. Federal legislature of the 13 colonies and then of the United States under the Articles of Confederation.

34. Unit of energy needed to raise the temperature of one gram of water one degree Centigrade.

35. Explorer born in Genoa who sailed to the Americas in 1492.

36. This Oscar-winning Humphrey Bogart/Ingrid Bergman film featured the song "As Time Goes By."

37. Music for small groups of instruments with one player for each part is called _____ music.

38. Method for painless diagnosis of the body, especially the brain. The machine creates a computerized image (two words).

39. Vulture that inhabits high mountains in southern California and in the Andes. It's the largest bird in existence.

40. A great silver lode mined in the 1800s in west Nevada, named after the man who claimed it.

41. Government work project for young men, founded in 1933 by Congress to provide jobs and job training in the field of natural resources (three words).

42. She's been in show biz for over 45 years. Her best-known stage work is *Hello, Dolly*.

43. Term given to a corporation with diversified operations due to buying out smaller companies.

44. Where King Arthur's palace and court were, popularized when President John F. Kennedy and his wife Jacqueline lived in the White House.

45. Style of music with a lively meter, originating in the West Indies.

46. Heavy, strong draft horse of a breed originating in Scotland.

47. This Chinese-American detective was created by novelist Earl Derr Biggers.

48. The national anthem for what country begins "Rush to combat, citizens of Bayamo"?

49. Archaeological site of a Mayan city in Mexico, a favorite tourist spot, with pyramids and temples.

50. This institution dates from the 12th century. Its members are chosen by the Pope as his aides and advisers (three words).

Score: _____ correct

D

Knowledge is of two kinds. We know
a subject ourselves, or we know
where we can get information upon
it.

Samuel Johnson

1. French writer best known for 20-year preparation of an encyclopedia of arts and sciences, of which the first volume was published in 1751.

2. Colorful paper cover for hardback books, _____ jacket.

3. A reading disorder of unknown cause that results in an individual, despite a good I.Q., finding it extremely difficult to learn to read.

4. Any number from 0 to 9.

5. The hardest natural substance known, a gemstone.

6. On the TV series "Charlie's Angels," this actor played the part of John Bosley.

7. A system of book classification used in libraries, using the numbers 000 to 999 to classify general topics, with decimals added to identify subtopics (three words).

8. After man, the most intelligent mammal (aquatic).

9. It has been described as half a dog high and two dogs long.

10. Fantasy board game popular among young adults (three words).

11. English writer whose novel, based on the true-life experience of Alexander Selkirk, who was cast away on a desert island, became a classic.

12. Surname of one-time dictator of Haiti; Papa Doc's rule was a reign of terror.

13. Famous collection of 100 short stories written by Giovanni Boccaccio (witty and sometimes X-rated).

14. Wild dog of Australia that preys on small animals and livestock.

15. Although her real name was Elizabeth Gilmer, she adopted this pen name in writing an advice column for women for a New Orleans newspaper. The column was appearing in 273 newspapers by 1940.

16. Small Old World rodent, one of the guests at the Mad Hatter's Tea Party.

17. Marie, Yvonne, Annette, Cecile, and Emilie (two words).

18. Hugh Lofting introduced this well-loved character in letters to his children, then went on to write many stories about him. Rex Harrison played the character's part in a movie about the search for the Pink Snail (two words).

19. Spanish explorer who led a party that discovered the Mississippi River in 1541. He died during the journey and was buried in that river.

20. Lovable Walt Disney elephant.

21. The medieval French called this common weed "lion's tooth," after its leaves.

22. Town in Greece, near the foot of Mount Parnassus, where a temple housed a famous and powerful oracle.

23. Unit of sound strength, represented by the symbol dB.

24. Members of the A.I.D. used to be called interior decorators. Now they are called interior _____.

25. This heavy, flightless bird, about the size of a turkey, is now extinct. It once inhabited the island of Mauritius. The term is also used to describe something way behind the times.

26. The plural is dice. What is the singular?

27. One who searches for water with some sort of divining rod.

28. This bird is the emblem of peace.

29. Where a misbehaving husband might be, in his wife's view (slang).

30. Computer slang for finding and correcting errors or malfunctions in computer programs.

31. Madam _____ was always knitting in Dickens's *Tale of Two Cities*.

32. French word meaning "relaxation," used politically to refer to the easing of tensions between the U.S. and the Soviet Union.

33. A number system in which $9 + 3 = 0$.

34. Vampire from Transylvania in book written by Bram Stoker.

35. Capital of the first state to enter the Union.

36. Ancient priests who held their rites in oak groves.

37. Double-helix structure that can make exact copies of itself.

38. An athletic contest featured in the Olympics that includes ten events.

39. Region between the equator and the trade wind zones, where winds are light, storms violent, and navigation difficult.

40. Pythias was saved from execution in the 4th century B.C. by this good friend.

41. A French inventor discovered the process of photography resulting in this type of portrait, fixed on a plate of copper coated with silver.

42. This male bee has no sting and gathers no honey.

43. This site (two words) in the Sierra Nevada is named after families en route to California in the 1800s who were trapped by heavy snow before reaching their destination. They resorted to cannibalism to survive.

44. Slang for an American infantryman in World War I.

45. Some camels carry heavy loads and are referred to as luggage camels. What are camels called that are ridden?

46. What D.D. stands for after a name.

47. A garbage can in Britain.

48. A door divided in two horizontal sections so that the upper part can be opened while the lower part stays closed (two words).

49. Country ruled by Queen Margrete. The monetary unit here is the krone.

50. Surname of German artist whose *Praying Hands* has been reproduced in many low-cost decorative items for the home.

Score: _____ correct

E

Knowledge is the only instrument of production that is not subject to diminishing returns.

J. M. Clark

1. Surname of founder of the Christian Science movement.

2. Large flightless bird of Australia, related to the ostrich.

3. Genus that includes the horse, zebra, and donkey. Also the title of a psychological thriller starring Richard Burton.

4. Island in the Tyrrhenian Sea where Napoleon was exiled after he was defeated.

5. A recording of the electrical activity of the brain.

6. This member of French royalty, a beautiful Spanish-born lady, was consort to Napoleon III.

7. Dangerous fish because it can discharge 400 volts of electricity (two words).

8. Town in Uganda where, in 1976, Israeli commandos flew in to rescue 91 passengers aboard a hijacked plane.

9. John Steinbeck novel, made into a movie starring James Dean and Julie Harris, about a sensitive youth who feels unloved.

10. What the superscript 2 is called in the expression 6^2.

11. Alpine plant with white floral leaves and yellow flowers, protected by law in Switzerland; the subject of a song in *The Sound of Music*.

12. Artificial language developed by L. L. Zamenhof of Poland in 1887. Its spelling is phonetic and the grammar is simple.

13. Large freshwater marsh covering 5,000 square miles of southern Florida, home of abundant wildlife.

14. An aboriginal people native to Siberia, but now found also in Alaska, Canada, and Greenland.

15. Term coined by French philosopher Jean-Paul Sartre to name his ideas of man's responsibility to control his own destiny.

16. Knowledge obtained from beyond the five senses, such as telepathy.

17. Polynesian island celebrated for its unusual hieroglyphs and colossal carved heads, some weighing over 50 tons, so named because of the day it was discovered in 1722.

18. Surname of famed Irish patriot, hanged for treason after leading an attack on Dublin Castle in 1803. Irish poet Thomas Moore wrote about this man's love affair in two poems.

19. Takes place the first Tuesday after the first Monday in November.

20. The vernal _____ is around March 21, the autumnal is around September 23. These are the times when night and day are 12 hours each everywhere in the world.

21. The center of a tropical hurricane, where only light winds prevail.

22. King Arthur's sword.

23. A wave signal reflected back to its point of origin from a distant object; a nymph in Greek mythology.

24. Novel by William Peter Blatty about a young girl possessed by demons, made into a movie starring Linda Blair.

25. The capital of Scotland.

26. In the Bible, the mother of Cain, Abel, and Seth.

27. The opposite of UHF (radio frequency).

28. In Einstein's famous equation $E = mc^2$, what the E stands for.

29. A short, pointed saying.

30. One who starts his own business or other enterprise in which some initiative and often risk is inherent.

31. Part of a river with mixed salt and fresh water due to ocean tides. The Hudson River is such.

32. A structure 984 feet tall, for many years the tallest monument in the world. It was built in Paris for the 1889 World's Fair.

33. The major river in southwest Asia. It provides irrigation through a wide flood plain to Syria and Iraq.

34. Surname of aviatrix who, in 1932, flew alone from Newfoundland to Ireland, the first woman's transatlantic solo. She disappeared in 1937 on a flight around the world.

35. Charles Darwin's theory on this subject caused great controversy between scientists and the clergy.

36. Annual awards sponsored by the Academy of Television Arts and Sciences for best nighttime programming.

37. This fur comes from the weasel, also called the stoat, and is associated with royalty.

38. First word in title of poem by Thomas Gray, written in 1750, from which this is a quote: "The curfew tolls the knell of parting day/ The lowing herd wind slowly o'er the lea."

39. The highest mountain in the world, in the Himalayas.

40. The study of insects.

41. What mediums call the materialization of a spirit.

42. U.S. dollars circulated among European banks and other European lending institutions, usually for short-term trade financing.

43. Round red cheese that originates in a town of the same name in the Netherlands.

44. Imaginary circle around the earth, midway between the North and South Poles.

45. What Archimedes supposedly shouted while running down the street naked.

46. Name of the first American satellite, launched in 1958.

47. Surname of first woman to swim the English channel, in 1926.

48. The evergreen tree that is the only food of the koala.

49. A method for moving people up and down in buildings. When first installed at Harrods of London, brandy was provided for passengers who might feel faint while riding on it.

50. Memento of the bull presented to an honored guest at a bullfight after a bull has been killed by the matador.

Score: _____ correct

F

Personally, I'm always ready
to learn, although I do not
always like being taught.
                Winston Churchill

1. Semicircular window over a door.

2. Amateur-produced magazine for a subculture such as sci-fi devotees.

3. What the *F* stands for in reference to an AF camera.

4. Slang term for a receiver of stolen goods.

5. Foot-stomping Spanish dance.

6. French army officer who became commander in chief of all Allied armies, including the American, during the First World War.

7. Weapons used for this sport include the foil, the épée, and the saber.

8. Only you can prevent them, according to Smokey the Bear (two words).

9. A flourish of trumpets.

10. Opera by Charles Gounod about one who sold his soul to the devil.

11. Term used for the plant and animal life of a specific area (three words).

12. This novel by Mary Shelley, written in 1818, has been the basis for countless horror movies.

13. Radioactive dust lingering after atomic and nuclear explosions.

14. Floral symbol used in the coat of arms of the royal house of France.

15. Those who took part in the California Gold Rush after gold was discovered there in the 1880s.

16. Member of a religious order; a monk.

17. "Where the poppies blow between the crosses, row on row" (two words).

18. Surname of designer of a German pursuit plane used in World War I. Later he came to the U.S. and designed planes for this country.

19. Surname of twins Esther Pauline and Pauline Esther, born in Sioux City, Iowa. Both became syndicated columnists.

20. British colony seized by Argentina in 1982, but won back by the British after a relatively short skirmish.

21. She taught cooking, but her fame rests on the cookbook she produced at the Boston Cooking School.

22. "Oi Maamme Suomi Synnylumaa" is the national song of what country?

23. A computer language; also known as formula translation.

24. Democrats' slogan during the Presidential election campaign of 1844, referring to a dispute with Great Britain over the Oregon territory.

25. Surname of German-Dutch physicist who first used mercury in a thermometer and devised a temperature scale.

26. A spirit, often appearing as an animal, attending a witch or demon.

27. Principles offered by President Roosevelt as the basis for peace in the world. They are now part of the U.N. charter.

28. What Nero is alleged to have done while Rome burned.

29. He remarked, "I am a _____, not a Lincoln" on becoming Vice President in 1973.

30. In 1790 a steamboat designed by this man (surname) carried paying passengers between Trenton and Philadelphia.

31. A dangerously attractive woman, from the French (two words).

32. June 14th, _____ Day.

33. French monetary unit (also in some other European countries).

34. U.S. Supreme Court Justice from 1939 to 1962. He helped to found the American Civil Liberties Union.

35. Cat that was the hero of animated film cartoons in the 1920s.

36. Tempus _____.

37. Ballroom dance popular in the U.S. from the 1920s to the 1950s, alternating slow and quick steps.

38. The term *jetsam* refers to things thrown overboard from a ship. What is the word for goods found floating on the sea?

39. Fifteen-letter word signifying a flighty, frivolous person.

40. Staple food item at fast-food chains (two words).

41. Term meaning the paid employment of a worker whose work is not necessary, as when technology replaces a person, but he is kept on anyway.

42. A deliberately unnatural, high-pitched voice.

43. Quakers.

44. What Izaak Walton wrote about.

45. A round stiff hat, usually red with a black tassel, that used to be the national headdress of the Turks.

46. Dish of hot dip with bread or crackers.

47. A small fast ship, usually armed, of the late 18th and early 19th century.

48. An arm of the North Sea in Scotland (three words).

49. Long-legged wading bird with a long neck and pink or rosy-red feathers.

50. Another name for the lightning bug.

Score: _____ correct

G

It was said of one of the most intelligent men who ever lived in New England, that when asked how he came to know so much about everything, he replied, By constantly realizing my own ignorance, and never being afraid or ashamed to ask questions.

Tryon Edwards

1. The site of meridian longitude 0°, ruling the time zones.

2. Role made famous by Marlon Brando as Mafia bigwig in 1972 movie.

3. Dorothy Parker wrote that men seldom make passes at girls who wear these.

4. Wall scribblings such as "Kilroy was here"; from the Italian for the word *scratchings*.

5. Popular name for the paper currency, not backed by gold or silver, issued by the Federal government during the Civil War.

6. This device was used to chop off the heads of thousands of Frenchmen during the French Revolution.

7. Largest island in the world; about four-fifths of it is covered by an ice cap.

8. Long suspension bridge built across the entrance of San Francisco Bay (two words).

9. Illustrator Charles Dana Gibson created this "ideal woman" of the time (two words).

10. Great desert, high in central Asia, 500,000 square miles.

11. Australian feminist, author of *The Female Eunuch*, and a teacher of literature.

12. "Thank you" in Spanish.

13. Surname; his most repeated quote is "Go west, young man."

14. She starred in the 1942 movie *Mrs. Miniver*, about the courage of the British during the bombings of World War II.

15. Breed of dairy cattle developed in the Channel Islands, producing rich milk.

16. Mythical creature, half bird and half beast, often used as a gargoyle.

17. What the inhabitants of Brobdindnag were in Swift's *Gulliver's Travels*.

18. Small freshwater fish. Males are favored in aquariums because of their vivid coloring.

19. Island of the Southwest Pacific Ocean where heavy fighting occurred between the U.S. and Japan in World War II.

20. Surname of French painter who died in poverty. His life was the subject of the book *The Moon and Sixpence*, by Somerset Maugham.

21. Soup made from okra, often with meat and vegetables.

22. For years, before the laws were changed, this Scottish town, just across the border from England, was where young eloping English couples went to be married (two words).

23. What the "lead" in lead pencils is.

24. Early in February each year, this hibernating animal leaves his burrow, according to legend, to see whether the sun is shining.

25. In a tale by Dr. Seuss, somebody stole Christmas. It was the _____.

26. Original name of the Girl Scouts when they were founded in 1912.

27. The strait a vessel traverses to get from Spain to Morocco.

28. American public-opinion statistician. He founded the American Institute of Public Opinion.

29. The angel considered the herald of good tidings in the New Testament.

30. Town in Pennsylvania where Confederate soldiers were defeated by Federal forces during the Civil War (1863).

31. Wildebeest, known by another name in crossword puzzles.

32. Composer from a Jewish immigrant family who wrote successful songs and musical compositions during the 1920s and 1930s, including *Rhapsody in Blue*.

33. Pitman is one system. Name the other, better known.

34. The official language of Ireland.

35. Because of its odd appearance, Europeans theorized that the parents of this animal were a camel and a leopard.

36. Surname of Soviet diplomat, ambassador to the U.S. from 1943–46. He helped arrange summit talks in the seventies between the U.S. and the Soviet Union.

37. Slang term for a woman interested only in a man's money.

38. These brothers collected folk and fairy tales that have delighted children for generations.

39. Rodent that looks like a mouse and hops like a kangaroo; often kept as a pet.

40. That part of a chromosome that transfers characteristics from parent to offspring.

41. A protein in blood plasma that contains antibodies.

42. A collection of billions of stars held together by gravity but separated from other star systems by vast space.

43. What plaster of Paris, used for casts and wallboard, is made from.

44. This plant is related to the pumpkin, cucumber, and watermelon, and is often used in decorative arrangements.

45. Coffee-exporting country in Central America. Its capital was Antigua until the city was destroyed by earthquakes in 1779. The new capital bears the same name as the country.

46. Novel by F. Scott Fitzgerald, written in 1922, about the corruption of the American dream (two words).

47. Pope in the 1500s, best known for the reformed calendar which was given his name.

48. In Germany, a secondary school. In the U.S., a room designed for physical education.

49. Apache Indian chief who led repeated raids against the whites.

50. Italian astronomer said to have constructed the first astronomical telescope.

Score: _____ correct

H

Anyone who stops learning is old,
whether at 20 or 80. Anyone who
keeps learning stays young. The
greatest thing in life is to keep
your mind young.

Henry Ford

1. Musical instrument with a keyboard, now superseded by the piano.

2. The Father of Medicine, Greek physician whose name is given to the Oath.

3. An inert gas used widely for balloons and airships; one of the periodic elements.

4. Primate with a large brain; it walks upright.

5. An air-cushion vehicle, so called because it floats on a cushion of air and does not touch the ground as it travels.

6. Game played with a ball and sticks between two teams of 11 players each.

7. Verse form borrowed from the Japanese, consisting of three unrhymed lines containing five, seven, and five syllables in that order.

8. Irish coins portray this musical instrument.

9. Capital city of Finland, where the Olympic Games were held in 1952.

10. Master magician, famous for his incredible escapes. His real name was Erich Weiss.

11. Eskimo dog used for pulling dogsleds.

12. A former mayor of Minneapolis, he went on to become U.S. Senator from Minnesota. He served as Vice President under Lyndon B. Johnson.

13. The strong tendons at the back of the human knee.

14. Old-fashioned reading primer containing the alphabet and religious material.

15. The First Lady of the American theater, wife of Charles MacArthur (two words).

16. Old Scottish meat dish originally cooked in a sheep's stomach. Today a plastic skin is often used.

17. Where the active volcano Mauna Loa is.

18. Hollywood gossip columnist of the thirties and forties, noted for her exotic hats (two words).

19. University of Cambridge, Massachusetts, the oldest American college.

20. Home of Andrew Jackson, east of Nashville.

21. A first-aid method to relieve choking, named after the doctor who popularized it.

22. One's code name in C.B. talk.

23. Socrates died from drinking a potion made from this poisonous plant.

24. The four *H*'s in 4H stand for head, heart, hands, and _____.

25. The most famous of Greek heroes, he successfully completed the "12 labors," including cleaning the Augean stables.

26. Sudden uncontrollable contraction of the human diaphragm, which everyone has experienced.

27. Emperor of Japan, starting in 1926. Following the surrender of Japan in World War II, he renounced war and helped formulate a new constitution for his country.

28. Slang for bumpkin, yokel.

29. "_____ sometimes sleeps" meaning anyone, even the best, can make mistakes. The missing name is the author of the *Iliad* and the *Odyssey*.

30. Name for the knowledge of armorial bearings; the coat of arms.

31. Hero of a poem by Longfellow. He marries Minnehaha.

32. Unfortunate result the next morning of too much alcoholic indulgence.

33. Capital of the largest island in the West Indies. Large tobacco factories are here and a cigar is named after the city.

34. System of medical treatment which believes in tiny doses of a medication that would, in healthy persons, produce symptoms of the disease being treated.

35. An intellectual.

36. Surname of German composer best known for his opera *Hansel and Gretel*. His name was borrowed by singer Arnold Dorsey.

37. Surname of English authority on card games.

38. Ichabod Crane was pursued by him in Washington Irving's *The Legend of Sleepy Hollow* (two words).

39. Inherited blood disorder characterized by excessive bleeding; found in males but carried by females.

40. Surname of two different men: one a noted film director of suspense films, the other a cabinetmaker whose chairs are now collector's items.

41. Seat of government in the Netherlands.

42. Slang for an actor who overacts.

43. Went with a sickle in the Soviet Union.

44. One of the five Great Lakes.

45. One who is afflicted with imaginary illnesses.

46. A six-sided figure.

47. Symbol writing found in Egypt dating back thousands of years.

48. Spear with rope attached, used to hunt whales.

49. A three-dimensional picture made without a camera which can be viewed (with special lighting) from different angles.

50. Jewish holiday which falls in December.

Score: _____ correct

I

'Tis education forms the common mind,
Just as the twig is bent, the tree's inclined.
Alexander Pope

1. Aer Lingus is the airline for this country.

2. The soap that's 99⁴⁴/₁₀₀ percent pure.

3. The correct name for the huge research and education center in Washington, D.C., is "the Smithsonian _____."

4. Magicians produce them; so do mirages; so does trompe l'oeil.

5. The farthest distance to which a camera's focus may be set.

6. This long-legged, long-necked wading bird was sacred in ancient Egypt.

7. Wife of Ferdinand V of Castile. She helped Columbus.

8. Device by which a composite portrait of a criminal is drawn by a police artist using the descriptions of witnesses.

9. Nineteenth-century French school of painting.

10. Type of supersonic missile (acronym).

11. The ninth letter of the Greek alphabet, used in English to indicate a tiny amount.

12. Kind of triangle with two equal sides.

13. A deadlock, a situation with no way out.

14. Kind of light provided by ordinary light bulbs.

15. He tried to fly with wings of feathers and wax, but flew too high and the sun melted his wings.

16. Epic poem by Dante about hell.

17. Animal with more than one cell but no backbone, such as worms.

18. Egyptian goddess.

19. Informal promissory note.

20. It was responsible for the sinking of the *Titanic* in 1912.

21. World-famous auto race held in Indiana.

22. Attribute of silent film star Clara Bow, fad word for "sex appeal."

23. A conductor or manager of an opera or concert company.

24. A country of more than 3,000 islands in Asia, the main island being Java.

25. A common poetic meter.

26. The Mohammedan religion. The word means "submission to the will of Allah."

27. Indictment of U.S. President Andrew Johnson, but he was acquitted.

28. Indelible black ink used in drawing and lettering (two words).

29. Acronym for the international police. Headquarters are in Paris.

30. Element necessary for the healthy functioning of the thyroid gland.

31. Greek epic poem.

32. Militant industrial labor union disciplined by the U.S. government during World War I.

33. A hormone produced by the pancreas that regulates the body's use of sugar.

34. Egyptian architect who helped build the earliest pyramid.

35. French name for the Five Nations of Indians.

36. Where the Harry S. Truman Library and Museum are.

37. The colored part of the eye.

38. The 15th of March, May, July, and October on the ancient Roman calendar.

39. Mental age divided by real age times 100.

40. Phrase used by Winston Churchill to mean an impenetrable barrier (two words).

41. Musical term indicating an interlude in a musical work.

42. Lizard that can grow to 6 feet.

43. Manuscripts decorated with letters and art in color or gold and silver are referred to as _____.

44. TV series starring Raymond Burr as a gruff detective confined to a wheelchair.

45. Part of the psyche.

46. The higher atmosphere of the earth.

47. Scottish site where Macbeth murdered Duncan.

48. Member of advanced Indian culture in Peru before the Spanish conquest.

49. Novel by Sir Walter Scott about a knight who rescued Richard the Lion-Hearted.

50. Island republic in the North Atlantic. Reindeer can be found here.

Score: _____ correct

J K

Every man has a right to his opinion,
but no man has a right to be wrong in
his facts.

Bernard M. Baruch

---

1. New Zealand's national bird, also called the apteryx. It cannot fly and is a threatened and protected species.

2. Type of music native to the South, associated especially with New Orleans. It originated with American blacks.

3. Irish novelist and poet who used the stream-of-consciousness technique in his *Portrait of the Artist as a Young Man*.

4. Author of the novel *One Flew Over the Cuckoo's Nest*.

5. Rice cooked with ham, sausage, chicken, shrimp or oysters, and seasoned with herbs.

6. Site of the first English settlement in North America.

7. Africa's highest mountain, an extinct volcano.

8. The middle period of the Mesozoic era.

9. Japanese suicide pilots in World War II.

10. Actor, composer, writer, and Rhodes Scholar, he starred in *Semi-Tough* (surname).

11. The most powerful of felines, yellow-tan with black spots.

12. A Chinese god or idol.

13. The dictionary says this is a herbivorous leaping marsupial animal.

14. Rudolph Dirks created this comic strip featuring two mischievous small boys (two words).

15. The book of writings accepted by Muslims as holy, equivalent to our Bible.

16. Capital of Jamaica and largest town in the Caribbean, with a landlocked port.

17. Form of unarmed combat, developed as a less violent form of Japanese jujitsu.

18. Algonquin-speaking tribe of Indians, formidable warriors.

19. Outlaw, a member of William Quantrill's raiders in the Civil War.

20. Dustin Hoffman starred in this 1979 movie about an advertising man who discovers what raising a child means after his wife leaves them.

21. Musical instrument of the percussion family.

22. Capital of Nepal.

23. Area popularly believed to be in Alaska, but actually in the Yukon Territory, Canada; site of gold rush.

24. Muppet character.

25. Nautical miles per hour.

26. Secret society organized in the South, aimed at suppressing blacks (three words).

27. Wife of Ahab, King of Israel; woman of loose morals.

28. Civil rights leader and ordained minister who unsuccessfully ran for President.

29. Title of poem that begins " 'Twas brillig, and the slithy toves. . . ."

30. Abbreviation for the former Soviet State Security Committee.

31. Useful vehicle with four-wheel drive; gets its name from "general purpose vehicle."

32. Australian term for baby kangaroo.

33. To offer unasked advice to others playing cards.

34. A mental quirk that compels people to steal things they don't need.

35. Large airplane that can carry several hundred passengers (two words).

36. Orange-yellow citrus fruit.

37. Eskimo canoe.

38. Optical toy consisting of a tube into which one looks while rotating it. Bits of colored glass in the bottom form changing patterns with inner mirrors.

39. Word that sounds plural but is singular, meaning honor and praise.

40. Mechanical heart named after its inventor.

41. Bertie Wooster's valet.

42. Sanskrit term: the belief that how a man behaves in this life influences his next life.

43. German expression meaning a friendly coffee-and-conversation get-together.

44. South African gold coin.

45. Author of bicentennial series on Americana.

46. Superman's home planet; a colorless gas.

47. Trademark name for a small roly-poly baby doll.

48. Emperor who founded the Mongol dynasty in China.

49. Giant ape who kidnapped Fay Wray in 1933 film.

50. Computer lever.

Score: _____ correct

L

Learning makes a man fit company
for himself.

Thomas Fuller

1. Country-music singer whose life was the subject of a 1980 feature film starring Sissy Spacek.

2. Business term for goods advertised at below dealer price in order to attract customers (two words).

3. "O ye'll tak' the high road/and I'll tak' the low road..." is from the song _____.

4. What a truck is called in Britain.

5. Adjective describing children who carry a key to the house because their working parents won't be there when they get home from school.

6. Werewolf.

7. Nickname for the wife of President Lyndon Johnson.

8. 1920s slang referring to young men who fawn upon older women for money.

9. What tennis players call a score of zero.

10. Grease derived from wool, often used in lotions.

11. Paris landmark; art gallery and museum.

12. Celebrated actress of the 1880s, friend of the then Prince of Wales.

13. She is 151 feet tall and her 100th birthday was celebrated in 1986.

14. Controversial drug derived from apricot pits, sometimes used in the treatment of cancer.

15. Magnifying glass worn in the eye socket by jewelers.

16. The *Harvard* _____, America's oldest college humor magazine.

17. Device for light amplification by stimulated emission of radiation.

18. British Cunard liner that was sunk by the Germans during World War II before America entered the war.

19. Arrangement between the U.S. and its allies during World War II by which the U.S. agreed to provide services and supplies to the Allies.

20. Scottish explorer in Africa sought by H. M. Stanley.

21. Rodents found in northern and Arctic areas that migrate to the sea and drown.

22. Garden herb related to the onion; national emblem of Wales.

23. Worm with suckers at both ends, once used to bleed patients suffering from any illness.

24. Capital of Portugal.

25. Irish elf.

26. Bath sponge used for scrubbing, made from a gourd's inner network.

27. Superman's girl friend (two words).

28. Nickname given to Charles Lindbergh after he flew the first successful solo nonstop flight across the Atlantic (two words).

29. Lake in central Switzerland; noted tourist attraction.

30. Term for someone unused to sea travel.

31. German air force under the Nazis.

32. Town in France, a shrine visited by pilgrims seeking cures for illness and disease.

33. A false and malicious statement, written or printed, that injures someone's reputation.

34. Diseased beggar in the Bible parable about the wealthy man and the beggar.

35. Stringed musical instrument of ancient Greece.

36. Beautiful gray horse used in exhibitions of dressage.

37. Legendary siren who lured sailors to their death with her singing.

38. International organization of insurance underwriters with headquarters in England.

39. Five-line verse, often rakish, with *aabba* rhyming scheme.

40. Roman numeral for 50.

41. A measurement of distance amounting to about 6 trillion miles.

42. The principle of noninterference, from the French, used particularly to refer to nonintervention by the government in economic affairs.

43. American inventor of the Polaroid camera (surname).

44. Sleight of hand.

45. Brain surgery inflicted on Jack Nicholson in *One Flew Over the Cuckoo's Nest*.

46. Baseball organization for players 8 to 12 years of age (two words).

47. Method of printing in which raised type is inked and impressed upon the surface of the paper.

48. Knight of the Holy Grail in old German legend. The story was made into an opera by Wagner.

49. Unit of currency in Italy.

50. Shakespearean comedy with alliterative title.

Score: _____ correct

M

Not to know is bad; not to wish
to know is worse.

African proverb

1. What they called those who left the Republican party in 1884.

2. Italian educator who gave her name to an educational philosophy stressing the independence and initiative of the child.

3. 1976 film about double agents and aging Nazis, starring Dustin Hoffman, Laurence Olivier, and Roy Scheider.

4. Fundamentalist Christian political action organization led by evangelist Reverend Jerry Falwell.

5. Yellowish-red tropical fruit.

6. To join this group you must have a very high IQ.

7. In chemistry, what the symbol Mg stands for.

8. Secret organization of Irish-American miners in Pennsylvania in the 1800s (two words).

9. Biblical character who lived to the age of 969.

10. "You have the right to remain silent..."

11. Brothers who invented the hot-air balloon.

12. Confection made with crushed almonds, sugar, and egg white, and formed into little shapes.

13. What volunteer U.S. militiamen were called during the Revolutionary War.

14. Nickname for a member of the Unification Church.

15. "The medium is the message," said this educator with regard to communication.

16. Thickness of $1/1000$ of an inch.

17. Stiff, square, tasseled cap worn by the graduating class.

18. American anthropologist who wrote interesting observations on life in primitive societies.

19. Deep-planted enemy agent.

20. Jim Henson's creations.

21. Syllable chanted repetitively during meditation.

22. Belgian poet and dramatist, best remembered for his work *The Bluebird*.

23. Popular board game first marketed in the 1930s.

24. French statesman, elected President of France in 1981.

25. Dutch painter known for his geometric-design paintings.

26. Lace scarf worn over the head and shoulders by Spanish women.

27. The king with the golden touch in Greek mythology.

28. Short-haired housecat with no tail.

29. Device for sending computer data over a telephone line.

30. The three wise men who brought gifts to baby Jesus.

31. Largest bird that ever lived, up to 12 feet tall, long extinct.

32. Secret organization of Sicilian criminals.

33. Chinese dynasty famous for its arts.

34. Chinese game played with tiles of ivory and bamboo.

35. Religious sect founded by Joseph Smith.

36. Robin Hood's love.

37. Small, energetic animal native to India that can kill snakes as large as a cobra.

38. Sherlock Holmes's archenemy.

39. A number that expresses the ratio of flight speed to the speed of sound.

40. The little people in *The Wizard of Oz*.

41. Author and lecturer who incurred the wrath of feminists when her book *The Total Woman* was published.

42. Offspring of a male donkey and a mare.

43. Signaling system using dots and dashes.

44. Baseball player with New York Yankees who hit 536 home runs.

45. English economist best known for his theory that the earth's population will exceed food supplies if population is not held in check (surname).

46. Wayland Flowers's dowager puppet.

47. Mascot for the Army military academy team.

48. Detroit-based record company.

49. Famous artist, painter, sculptor, poet, and architect. His sculpture *Pietà* is in St. Peter's, Rome.

50. Female detective in Agatha Christie novels.

Score: _____ correct

N

It is wise to get knowledge and
learning from every source—from
a sot, a pot, a fool, a winter-
mitten, or an old slipper.

François Rabelais

1. In music, a piece for nighttime, something dreamy, soothing, romantic.

2. Variety of peach with no fuzz.

3. Star whose brightness increases dramatically within a short time, a few hours or a few days. This unusual brightness is only temporary.

4. Kind of embroidery worked on canvas with a blunt needle.

5. U.S. citizen of Japanese descent.

6. Where one does not carry coals to.

7. Coin-collector.

8. Nickname for enormous sea serpent said to be living in Loch Ness, Scotland.

9. What the N stands for in NOW checking accounts.

10. Slang for government narcotics agent.

11. Favoritism given a relative over others, especially in job hiring.

12. Harbor city in the state of Virginia with one of the largest shipbuilding plants in the world.

13. Capital of Kenya.

14. The first nuclear-powered submarine, built in 1955. In 1958 it made the first voyage under the polar ice cap.

15. Handsome youth in Greek mythology who became enamored of his own reflection in the water.

16. Where the trial of Nazi leaders was conducted after World War II.

17. How the Russians say "no" (English spelling).

18. What Poe's raven said.

19. A short story or shorter-than-usual novel.

20. What the Japanese call Japan.

21. Modern-day follower of Hitler's philosophies.

22. Town in Israel in Galilee, where Jesus spent his early years.

23. International military defense organization, established in 1949.

24. That point in the sky opposite the zenith; lowest point.

25. Halo or other circle of light around the head of a sacred being.

26. Two words, slang; a timid person or one who is worrying without much reason.

27. Surname of Swedish philanthropist who founded annual awards for outstanding contributions to physics, chemistry, medicine, literature, economics, and peace.

28. A great king of Babylon who reputedly built the Hanging Gardens.

29. Term first used by Russian novelist Turgenev, meaning that morality is of no consequence and that societal institutions are corrupt and may rightfully be overthrown.

30. Prehistoric man, named after place near Dusseldorf, Germany, where bones of the species were found in 1856.

31. When a map was being drawn for this Alaskan seaport, it was noted that the cape at this point had no name. The entry was misread, and the misreading became the basis for the town's official name.

32. Home of country music.

33. Popular ballet and concert suite by Tchaikovsky.

34. Explosive liquid used in making dynamite; also used in medicine to relax or dilate blood vessels.

35. Relatively new concept of exchanging information and help informally among members of a group as a supportive measure.

36. Sixteenth-century French astrologer and physician who wrote a book of vague prophecies, many of which have come true.

37. A soft, light cheese similar to cream cheese but with less fat.

38. Drink of the ancient Greek and Roman gods.

39. Synthetic material used for, among other things, nightgowns, women's hosiery, and hairbrushes.

40. Word coined by George Orwell in *1984*, referring to a way of speaking in which an official says one thing that appears to mean another.

41. Russian actress who emigrated to the U.S. and became a noted Ibsen interpreter. She died in 1945.

42. Early movie theater offering silent films with piano accompaniment for a nickel.

43. Small bird of the thrush family. The male's song is most melodious.

44. French emperor; pastry with cream filling; card game; former French gold coin.

45. Slang term for criticism over matters too trivial to merit such attention.

46. Antibiotic used especially for skin infections.

47. The first atomic bomb ever used was dropped on Hiroshima. A few days later, a second atomic bomb was dropped on this Japanese city.

48. Greek goddess of retribution and vengeance.

49. Egyptian queen, wife of Pharaoh Akhenaton (Amnehotep IV), 18th dynasty.

50. Surname; author of these lines: "The wind was a torrent of darkness among the gusty trees/The moon was a ghostly galleon tossed upon cloudy seas..."

Score: _____ correct

It is better to know nothing than to know what ain't so.

Josh Billings

1. Pointed pillar with four sides, like Cleopatra's Needle.
2. Semiprecious iridescent stone.
3. Japanese sash.
4. Ape with long arms.
5. Large lake in Florida north of the Everglades.
6. Official who acts as liaison between the government and a complaining citizen.
7. M.D. who deals with eye problems.
8. Popeye's lady (two words).
9. Japanese art of folding paper into decorative shapes.
10. One kind of tea.
11. Town in Bavaria where a Passion play is performed.
12. One who studies birds and their behavior.
13. Statuette awarded yearly for achievements in motion pictures.
14. Last letter of the Greek alphabet.
15. Small, simple wood instrument with a mouthpiece and finger holes.
16. King of the fairies in *Midsummer Night's Dream*.
17. Jungle animal resembling a leopard.
18. Stone resembling marble, with varying colors in layers.
19. An English university and a shoe.
20. Herb used for seasoning, especially in Italian cookery.
21. A group of low mountains running through Missouri, Arkansas, and Oklahoma.
22. Call made by court officer to gain attention.
23. The capital of Norway.
24. Path of any object in space around a celestial body.
25. Disparaging nickname for a native of Oklahoma.
26. Overland pioneer route, about 2,000 miles long, from Independence, Missouri, to the Columbia River in Oregon. It was used in the 1700s and 1800s (two words).

27. Bright constellation outlining a hunter with belt and sword.

28. Bird said to put its head in the sand when pursued, in the belief that if it cannot see the enemy, the enemy cannot see it.

29. Marine creature with eight arms, living primarily at the bottom of the sea.

30. First woman member of the Supreme Court (surname).

31. Conflict over this commodity led to war between Britain and China in 1839.

32. King of Norway who succeeded to the throne upon the death of his father in 1957.

33. Superstition says you should eat these only in months with an *R* in them.

34. Branch of surgery dealing with problems of bones and muscles.

35. The one who sees the glass as half full.

36. American markswoman who performed in Buffalo Bill's Wild West show (surname).

37. Current slang indicating achieving superiority over another.

38. Trademarked board with movable planchette that spells out words, supposedly directed by spirits.

39. Figure of speech in which contradictory expressions are combined, as "make haste slowly."

40. King of gods in Norse mythology.

41. Symbol O, atomic number 8, the most abundant of all elements.

42. Member of a secret society originating in northern Ireland in 1795 to defend British rule and Protestantism.

43. A carnivore is a flesh-eating animal; an herbivore is a plant-eating animal. What is the term for an animal that eats both plants and meat?

44. Article of men's clothing, called dungarees in Britain. What are they called in the U.S.?

45. Musical composition of solo voices, chorus, and orchestra, but with no scenery.

46. Independent state in southeast Arabia, an absolute monarchy. Oil provides most government revenue.

47. Event whose flag displays five rings of color: black, blue, red, green, and yellow.

48. African animal related to the giraffe, with zebra-striped legs and hindquarters.

49. Fertile area in a desert.

50. Workplace of the President of the United States (two words).

Score: _____ correct

P Q

Informed people make wise decisions.
Wendell Wilkie

1. What a phrase such as "Madam, I'm Adam" is called.

2. Slang for one who passes bad checks.

3. A collection of buildings massed together that shelters the U.S. Department of Defense in Arlington, Virginia.

4. Legendary bird that sets fire to itself and then rises from the ashes to live again.

5. Color of the cow that Gelett Burgess said he never wanted to see.

6. A supernatural and mischievous force supposed to be responsible for dishes falling off shelves, knocking and rappings on walls, and other similar unexplained happenings.

7. Slang for the little finger.

8. Fudge made with brown sugar, butter, milk, and nuts.

9. 3.1416.

10. What real men supposedly never eat.

11. The 18th Amendment to the Constitution dealt with this.

12. U.S. Army officer in charge of general supplies.

13. What the *P* in EPCOT stands for.

14. Card game in which the best hand is a royal flush.

15. A traitor to one's country is referred to by this term, after a Norwegian who betrayed Norway to the Nazis.

16. Telephone switchboard in private use, as in a large office (abbrev.).

17. Brazilian soccer player (nickname).

18. Golden or pale cream-colored horse with lighter mane and tail.

19. Lie detector.

20. The last of these birds, known for their long migrations, died in a zoo in 1914 (two words).

21. The hunchback of Notre Dame in Victor Hugo's novel.

22. Method of painting developed by Georges Seurat and Paul Signac, using dots of color that blend together from a distance.

23. The bird about which it was written that "his bill can hold more than his belican."

24. Small electronic device implanted in patient's chest to stimulate and control heart action.

25. Court-ordered payment of an allowance from one member of an unmarried couple, now separated, to the other.

26. The largest borough of New York City, on Long Island. Buildings dating back to the 1600s are found here.

27. Name that was given to the governing body of the Communist party in the Soviet Union.

28. Common name for mercury.

29. P. T. Barnum's first name.

30. Surname of the author of these famed words: "...and so to bed."

31. Two words: island with repetitive name in American Samoa.

32. Ling-Ling and Hsing-Hsing are two of these.

33. A source of intense radio activity, similar to a star; the most distant object in the universe known to man.

34. Leading twentieth-century artist. He worked in sculpture, ceramics, and painting and is famed for his creativity in such fields as cubism and fantasy.

35. Small but deadly fish found in South American waters.

36. Small game bird, such as the bobwhite.

37. Standard drug for treating malaria.

38. Upper deck of a ship from the mainmast to the stern.

39. Black woman who refused to give up her bus seat to a white man in 1955 (surname).

40. Marionette whose nose grew longer each time he told a lie.

41. Common mineral, a form of silica, found in crystal formations. Clocks and watches use these to drive the motor at a precise rate for accuracy.

42. Novel by Grace Metalious that became a bestseller.

43. Animal that is native to waters of Australia and Tasmania. It lays eggs and has webbed feet and a beak like a duck.

44. Home of the Liberty Bell.

45. Greek temple of Doric architecture on the Acropolis at Athens.

46. Depression that afflicts some women who have just given birth.

47. A square dance for four couples.

48. Author of *Common Sense* and *The Age of Reason*. His writings encouraged the Declaration of Independence.

49. Name given to the double-cut screwdriver.

50. Little girl in the *Peanuts* cartoons who plays baseball (two words).

Score: _____ correct

R

If a man empties his purse into his head,
no man can take it away from him. An investment
in knowledge always pays the best interest.

Benjamin Franklin

1. Serbian monk notorious for his bad influence over the Russian monarch.

2. Chesspiece or bird.

3. Coastal strip with many fashionable resorts, located between the Mediterranean Sea and the mountains.

4. Husband of Dale Evans.

5. He worked with Oscar Hammerstein in composing music for *The King and I*.

6. Where King John accepted the Magna Carta.

7. A letter circulated from one person to another in a group, with each adding comments (two words).

8. The bugle call or drum roll used in the armed forces to signal that it is time to get up.

9. Once the divorce capital of the world because of its quick and easy divorce laws.

10. Means of detecting the direction and range of aircraft and ships by the reflection of sound waves.

11. Twin brothers raised by a wolf; the legendary founders of Rome.

12. Popular name for the First Regiment of U.S. Cavalry Volunteers in the Spanish-American War.

13. R2D2 and C3PO.

14. Garden plant also called the pieplant; a fuss or a quarrel (slang).

15. Half of a diameter.

16. Series of inkblot patterns used in psychology to test patients.

17. The gigantic white bird in *Sinbad the Sailor*.

18. The first man to put together a book on parliamentary procedure (1876) (surname).

19. Politician who was once president of the Screen Actors Guild.

20. A parallelogram with oblique angles, of which opposite sides are equal and adjacent sides unequal.

21. Large evergreen tree, growing as high as 385 feet.

22. Pit viper, of which the diamondback is the largest and most deadly.

23. Game similar to football and soccer, originating in England.

24. City where the Mayo Clinic is located. It was named after a city in New York State.

25. River that divided Gaul from Italy; Caesar led his army across it, beginning a civil war.

26. British business magnate who made a fortune in the diamond fields of South Africa (surname).

27. First American woman in space (surname).

28. The first of these deluxe automobiles was dubbed the Silver Ghost.

29. The belief that when someone dies, his soul returns in some form to exist again.

30. What occurs when sunlight passes through raindrops and is split up into the colors of the visible spectrum.

31. Gypsy language.

32. Smugglers of illegal liquor from ship to shore.

33. Black stone discovered in Egypt in 1799 that was inscribed in three different scripts.

34. Nickname given to women factory workers during World War II.

35. This bird, a member of the cuckoo family, seldom flies, but runs rapidly along the ground.

36. A collection of quatrains by the Persian poet Omar Khayyám.

37. In the French R.S.V.P., what the *R* stands for.

38. International news agency based in London; one of the largest news agencies.

39. Architectural style that existed in Italy in the 15th and 16th centuries.

40. Capital of the Confederacy during the Civil War.

41. The capital of Iceland.

42. Dwarf in German fairy tale who spins flax into gold for a maiden on condition that she tell him his name or forfeit her first child to him.

43. Pasta formed into small packets of dough containing a filling such as meat or cheese.

44. Abbreviation for medical prescription.

45. American cartoonist who collected unusual facts.

46. Reply meaning "O.K.," to indicate that a radio message has been received and understood.

47. Nickname of the "Robin Hood of Scotland," written about by Sir Walter Scott.

48. Musical setting of a mass for the dead; dirge.

49. Albert, Otto, Charles, Alfred, and John founded the world's largest circus. Their surname:

50. What the tired businessman is saying when he tells you he is taking time off for some R & R.

Score: _____ correct

S

The learning and knowledge that we have is, at the most, but little, compared with that of which we are ignorant.

Plato

---

1. Carved engravings on ivory or bone, especially those made by American whalers.

2. June 21 or 22 is the date of this seasonal event in the Northern Hemisphere; the day the sun is furthest from the Equator (two words).

3. Japanese alcoholic beverage.

4. Hebrew word meaning "peace," offered as greeting or farewell.

5. Traditional outer garment of Hindu women.

6. Name given to all the waters of the world (two words).

7. King's wife who told stories for 1,001 nights in the *Arabian Nights Entertainments.*

8. Another name for the U.S. flag.

9. Navy construction battalion that builds naval shore facilities in combat areas.

10. Dog Star, the brightest star in the night sky.

11. Sign (abbr.) that theaters put up when no more seats are left but you may still buy a ticket and attend.

12. First artificial satellite in orbit.

13. Small, flat-bottomed boat with mat roofing, seen in Chinese waters.

14. Number of squares on a chess board.

15. Valuable caterpillar which feeds on the leaves of mulberry trees.

16. Massive group of stones arranged in a circle in the south of England.

17. Arachnid with strong claws and a poisonous stinger at the tip of its tail.

18. Invention by Cousteau that allows deep-sea divers to carry their own air supply.

19. Buildings of great height, sometimes reaching over 100 stories.

20. Gilbert's musical collaborator in *The Mikado* and *H.M.S. Pinafore* (surname).

21. City in Massachusetts where 19 so-called witches were hanged in 1692.

22. Language of ancient India, the basis of most modern Indian languages.

23. A signaling system holding the arms, or flags, in different positions to indicate letters of the alphabet.

24. Government program instituted to protect people from hardship due to loss of income in old age (two words).

25. On a pirate flag, it goes with crossbones.

26. The study and exploration of caves, popularly known as "spelunking."

27. People who collect these are called philatelists.

28. This was used in the days of horse-drawn vehicles to deliver mail and transport passengers.

29. Name for the planets, satellites, and other heavenly bodies within the sun's area of attraction.

30. Former name of Ho Chi Minh City.

31. What follows ETOAIN.

32. Two slices of bread with meat in the middle, named after what nobleman?

33. American golfer; in the PGA Hall of Fame.

34. Title of a 1962 book by Rachel Carson about pollution of the environment (two words).

35. He shot Robert F. Kennedy in Los Angeles in 1968.

36. Abbreviation for tests given to high-school students by the College Board to determine their ability to do well in college.

37. Dancer who supposedly danced so beautifully that, at her request, Herod gave her the head of John the Baptist.

38. Award to championship ice hockey team after best-of-seven games series. Canadian teams often win, but U.S. teams have also claimed the trophy.

39. Author of the Song of Songs, third King of Israel, son of David.

40. Two-masted sailing ship.

41. Latin for "Holy of Holies"; used to refer to a place to go to where one won't be disturbed and things will not be interfered with (two words).

70/ S   NORMA GLEASON

42. Mineral deposits found hanging like icicles in caves.

43. A sect of Adventists who seceded from the Quakers. Their furniture is admired for its simple, functional design.

44. Instrument used to detect and record serious ground movements such as earthquakes.

45. A lyric poem of 14 lines. The form has been used by Shakespeare, Keats, and Wordsworth.

46. Branch of the U.S. Treasury that guards high executive officers.

47. Slang for a ten-dollar bill.

48. U.S. military decoration awarded for gallantry in action (two words).

49. Cross-shaped design adopted by Hitler as the Nazi emblem.

50. Irishman's club or cudgel.

Score: _____ correct

T

Alexander the Great so valued learning
that he used to say he was more indebted
to Aristotle for giving him knowledge than
to his father Philip for giving him life.
Thomas Babington Macaulay

1. South African province known for its gold fields. Diamonds are also an important mineral resource here.

2. Religious doctrine founded in 1875 by Mme. Blavatsky. It includes a belief in repeated reincarnations on ever higher levels.

3. Three-pronged spear carried by the sea god, Neptune.

4. Fencing term meaning a hit or touch.

5. One of those who supported the British during the American Revolution; also the popular name of a political party in Britain.

6. Jungle hero created by Edgar Rice Burroughs.

7. Stylized emblem of the Girl Scouts; cloverleaf.

8. Charles Sherwood Stratton was known by this nickname (two words, sometimes three words). He was three feet, four inches tall.

9. Tidal wave produced by underwater earthquakes or volcanic eruption, found chiefly in the Pacific.

10. Upside down (two words).

11. The cube root of 27.

12. Roly-poly brothers in *Alice in Wonderland*.

13. Island off the Asian mainland in the Pacific. It used to be called Formosa, is now officially the Republic of China.

14. What "demain" (French), "Morgen" (German), and "domani" (Italian) mean in English.

15. "Peter Piper picked a peck of pickled peppers" is one.

16. Famous archaeological site identified by the German archaeologist Heinrich Schliemann in 1870.

17. Nursery-rhyme character who trades a song for a meal.

18. The body of Jewish scripture, sacred writings, and rituals.

19. New York City jewelry store, begun in 1837. The store invested heavily in diamonds when prices were very low, sold them later at a huge profit. There are now branches in Paris, London, and Geneva.

20. State in southeast Mexico, from which comes the name of a popular hot sauce made from peppers.

21. Common vegetable, actually a fruit, that used to be called a "love apple."

22. Indian chief who led an Indian alliance against the whites but was defeated by General William Henry Harrison.

23. These flowers became a craze in the 1600s in Europe. People would pay large sums for rare varieties.

24. British university professor who wrote fantasy tales about Middle Earth (surname).

25. Small bloodsucking African fly. Its bite causes sleeping sickness that is often fatal.

26. This great British passenger ship was termed "unsinkable" when she was built, yet she sank on her maiden voyage.

27. Prophetic playing cards used in occult circles.

28. Shrubs or hedges clipped into ornamental shapes such as animals.

29. Private college founded by Booker T. Washington in 1881.

30. Underground fungus considered a delicacy. Pigs sniff them out.

31. Country, formerly called Siam; a kingdom in southeast Asia.

32. Famous waxworks museum in London.

33. His real name is Herbert Khaury. He married Miss Vicky and they had a child, Tulip (two words).

34. Prickly plant with flowers; the heraldic emblem of Scotland.

35. A heart-to-heart talk; intimate chat.

36. The letter that follows sigma in the Greek alphabet.

37. Companion to the vernacular Dick and Harry.

38. Pole set up by Native American Indians in front of their dwellings; carved with figures and animals.

39. Nickname of a Democratic political machine in New York City that, during its heyday, grew corrupt.

40. Small grassy mound, as where Little Miss Muffet sat.

41. Physicist largely responsible for the development of the hydrogen bomb.

42. Hoped-for result when the drug scopolamine is administered.

43. Four-letter abbreviation recited gratefully by office workers as they put on their coats to go home at 5 P.M. on the last working day of the week.

44. Sedative and sleep-inducing drug, withdrawn just a few years after its introduction when it was discovered that it caused malformed limbs in the fetuses of pregnant women who took it.

45. English illustrator who drew the pictures for *Alice in Wonderland* (surname).

46. In law, a wrongful, but not criminal, act against a person or his property for which damages would be legally due.

47. Britain's first female Prime Minister (surname).

48. Largest U.S. labor union.

49. Nickname for Hollywood, suggesting showy, cheap, and trashy (two words).

50. High-pitched drum which can be tuned, beaten with the hands.

Score: _____ correct

U V

Fullness of knowledge always and necessarily means some understanding of the depths of our ignorance, and that is always conducive to both humility and reverence.

Robert A. Millikan

1. The patron of love, a saint until he was dropped from the liturgical calendar in 1969.

2. The adder is an example of a venomous snake family called _____.

3. Celestial body discovered by Sir William Herschel in 1781—the first discovery of its kind through a modern telescope.

4. Humorous term for women's undergarments.

5. U.N. organization that offers help to children all over the world.

6. C, D, and K, for example.

7. Northernmost province of Ireland, now divided between the Republic of Ireland and Northern Ireland.

8. Moving object seen in the sky whose appearance and movement cannot be easily explained (abbrev.).

9. Scandinavian pirates of long ago.

10. At one time, member of lowest caste in India. A film of the same name about a federal agent (Eliot Ness) was made in 1987.

11. Sound beyond ordinary human hearing due to its very high frequency.

12. Heavy radioactive metallic element, the main source of nuclear energy.

13. Seat of the papal government of the Roman Catholic Church (two words).

14. Animated corpse that rises from the grave at night to suck the blood of living persons.

15. Religious denomination resulting from the merger of two churches. They believe reason and conscience, not creed, should govern human behavior.

16. Active volcano in Italy that often erupts.

17. The lower chambers of the heart.

18. What Julius Caesar said to announce his victory at Zela (three words).

19. Early Italian navigator and explorer (surname). A bridge in New York City is named after him.

20. Mythical animal resembling a horse, with a single horn in the middle of its forehead.

21. Ray beyond the end of the colors in the visible spectrum, on the short wavelength end.

22. Resort city in France; highly popular because of its natural hot springs; most famous as seat of collaborationist French government.

23. German submarine.

24. Prestigious institution of higher learning for women at Pough-keepsie, New York.

25. French landscape painter of street scenes (surname).

26. What nature abhors.

27. Animal native to South America, a relative of the llama, bred for its wool.

28. French for "you."

29. Diacritical mark used in the German language over some vowels.

30. Religion practiced in Haiti. Its rituals include magic and going into trances.

31. Bone on the human forearm.

32. Grade of peerage in Great Britain ranking below an earl and above a baron.

33. Mountain chain in the USSR that separates Europe and Asia.

34. Climbing orchid, from the pods of which a flavoring is extracted.

35. Settlement on Baffin Bay, Greenland, home of an air force base.

36. Spectrographically produced voice pattern, sometimes used to trap criminals.

37. Where Valentine and Proteus hailed from in Shakespearean play.

38. East African republic, once under British rule. Its capital is Kampala.

39. Small songbird. Some species have "spectacles"—eye rings connected by a band.

40. a³ = _____ of a cube.

41. The Stradivarius is one.

42. French novelist, author of *Around the World in Eighty Days* (surname).

43. Scientist who deals with viruses and the diseases caused by them.

44. Professional auto racer, Indy Car National Champion 1970, 1983, 1985.

45. Fine-grained lambskin, kidskin, or calfskin used for writing paper or book binding.

46. Large bird of prey, such as the turkey buzzard and the condor.

47. Longest river in Europe, linking the White, Baltic, Caspian, Azov, and Black seas.

48. Dutch painter, born 1632. His *Woman With a Water Jug* hangs in the Metropolitan Museum of Art in New York City.

49. Germanic tribe who produced the last Gothic king of Spain, Roderick.

50. President Carter's Secretary of State (surname).

Score: _____ correct

W X

The true order of learning should be:
first, what is necessary; second, what
is useful; and third, what is ornamental.
Lydia Sigourney

1. The "good king" who "looked out on the Feast of Stephen/When the snow lay round about/Deep and crisp and even."

2. What Don Quixote tilted at.

3. Spanish Jesuit missionary who started a mission in Japan in 1549.

4. The universal solvent, H_2O.

5. Pillar of water, common in tropical zones, caused by intense, fast-moving, low-pressure system over the sea, like a tornado.

6. Balcony or observation deck with railing on a house facing the sea, for watchers of ships (two words).

7. English poet laureate, author of "I Wandered Lonely as a Cloud."

8. Mythical town described by Garrison Keillor, Lake _____.

9. In the acronym WASP, what the *W* stands for.

10. Woman who shocked Britain in the 1930s when she married King Edward VIII (maiden name).

11. Percussion instrument composed of a series of bars which are struck by small hammers.

12. Socrates' bad-tempered wife.

13. Small, kangaroolike Australian marsupial.

14. Trademark widely used to refer to any photocopy; such use is objected to by the makers of the specific photocopier, whose trademark name is thus misused.

15. Adopted surname of Malcolm Little, American Black Muslim leader who was murdered in 1965.

16. Yarns stretched lengthwise in a loom, crossed by the woof in the weaving process.

17. Painter (surname) whose portrait of his mother, seated, entitled *Arrangement in Grey and Black*, is often called by another name.

18. A tubular piece of cloth, often canvas, open at both ends, flown at an airfield to show wind direction.

19. Science fiction tale by H. G. Wells about Martians out to destroy Los Angeles (four words).

20. Beads made from shells, used instead of money by Indians in North America.

21. The store manager (surname) who squeezes the Charmin in the television commercial.

22. Abbreviation indicating size, found on clothing for those who are considerably overweight.

23. Site of the last battle of the Napoleonic wars in 1815.

24. Apartment building in Washington, D.C., that was involved in history-making events in 1972.

25. The 28th President of the U.S., a former president of Princeton University, awarded the Nobel Peace Prize in 1919.

26. Reference book listing names and short biographies of celebrities and influential persons (two words).

27. Literary character who said, "The time has come to talk of many things/of shoes—and ships—and sealing wax—of cabbages—and kings."

28. Unit of electrical power, equal to one joule per second, was named after this Scottish inventor.

29. Deer common to Yellowstone National Park and other areas of the western U.S. and Canada, commonly called the American elk.

30. The flute, oboe, clarinet, and bassoon are classified as this type of musical instrument.

31. Heavy, colorless, nearly inert gas used in some flash tubes.

32. She wrote *Little House on the Prairie* in 1935. A television series was based on this and other of her books.

33. Fine English pottery, usually with white relief figures on a pastel (often blue) background.

34. London locale of international tennis matches.

35. Companion to Blynken and Nod.

36. Figure of speech indicating absent-mindedness or daydreaming.

37. He ran through the town upstairs and downstairs in his nightgown.

38. Officer of a political party in Congress who maintains discipline and checks on voting and attendance.

39. Large gray dog with docked tail, used for bird and game hunting.

40. Title of Charles Lindbergh's account of his flight across the Atlantic.

41. Any word in advertising copy that removes responsibility for exaggerated or misleading claims in the same ad (two words).

42. High stone wall in Jerusalem where Jews gather for prayers (two words).

43. A boxer or wrestler between a lightweight and a middleweight.

44. Yale University singing group.

45. Doctor who was Sherlock Holmes's friend and assistant.

46. Name of Emmett Kelly's clown persona (two words).

47. New York columnist and radio reporter, noted for his fast-paced delivery. He died in 1972.

48. "_____ Matilda," Australia's national song.

49. Common name for the trachea.

50. Five of Kipling's "six honest serving men."

Score: _____ correct

Y Z

Try to know everything of something, and something of everything.

Henry Peter, Lord Brougham

1. Hindu philosophy involving the withdrawal of the senses from the outside world, for discipline physically and mentally.

2. Domesticated bovine animal with a hump, native to Asia.

3. Language based on German but including words from Hebrew and other languages, written in the Hebrew alphabet.

4. Popular summer squash with dark green skin, shaped like a cucumber.

5. In Chinese philosophy, the two principles that represent earth and female, heaven and male.

6. Young, upwardly mobile group interested in the good life and money.

7. National park established in 1890. It contains many peaks of the Sierra Nevada range, giant sequoia trees, and waterfalls.

8. A hand in bridge or whist in which there is no ace and no card higher than a 9.

9. Men's fashion of the forties, consisting of baggy trousers, a long coat, a flashy necktie, and a wide-brimmed hat (two words).

10. Word used to indicate some large, unspecified number, over a million.

11. Desert plant belonging to the lily family. Some are small trees, like the Joshua tree; others are shrubs or low-growing plants.

12. Popular showy garden flower, usually orange or yellow; the state flower of Indiana.

13. Longest river in Asia, located in China, over 3,000 miles long.

14. Imaginary belt in the heavens, divided into twelve sections.

15. Skullcap worn by Jewish males in the synagogue, especially by Orthodox and Conservative Jews.

16. In Greek mythology, the god of earth and sky, leader over all other gods.

17. Word of German origin meaning the spirit of the times, the general tone of an era.

18. In the ZIP code, what the *Z* stands for.

19. Site in the Crimea where Roosevelt, Churchill, and Stalin met to plot the defeat of Germany in World War II.

20. Term given to the time it takes the earth to make a complete orbit around the sun.

21. German optician who established a now internationally-known optical factory (surname).

22. This vegetable has thick tubers, is grown in Florida and a few adjoining states plus other tropical or subtropical climates.

23. Married name of a professional woman athlete of the 30s, 40s, and 50s. She won gold medals in Olympic Games, and was also a fine swimmer, golfer, billiard player, and baseball player.

24. Derogatory term for someone who always agrees with superiors, no matter what he really thinks (two words).

25. British term for the letter *Z*.

26. Toy consisting of two round blocks connected by a dowel pin, around which string is wound. Players can toss out and reel in the toy by means of the string.

27. Naval petty officer whose duties are generally clerical.

28. Dessert similar to custard and ice cream, made from curdled milk.

29. Tall mixed drink, made with rum, liqueur, and fruit juice; or a corpse revived by voodoo.

30. A thick, creeping perennial grass used in lawns, particularly in the South.

31. Shaggy ox native to Tibet.

32. Comic 1983 film starring Woody Allen as an oddball, able to change his appearance at will.

33. Former name for inlet of the North Sea in the Netherlands. Part of it is known today as Lake Ijsselmeer (two words).

34. Title of tale about a boy's love for a pet fawn, written by Marjorie Kinnan Rawlings.

35. Stringed musical instrument played with fingers and a pick.

36. English merchant born in the U.S. who made a fortune. A college was named in his honor at New Haven, Connecticut (surname).

37. Humanlike but brutish creatures in *Gulliver's Travels*.

38. African animal with striking striped coat.

39. Common mineral found in crystals or grains. A transparent variety is made into gems. The colorless stones resemble diamonds.

40. "Alas, poor _____, I knew him, Horatio."

41. Unit of money in Japan.

42. Oldest and largest national park in the U.S.

43. Type of airship or dirigible, named after a count.

44. Paper wasp with black body and yellow markings (two words).

45. Capital of Cameroun.

46. This astronomical observatory boasts an extremely large refracting telescope.

47. A cell formed by the joining of two gametes.

48. Hardy, popular evergreen tree.

49. That point in the sky directly above the viewer; the highest point.

50. Pueblo Indian tribe.

Score: _____ correct

Section II
Challenge!

If you did well on Section I and feel quite superior, here is a further challenge. This special section contains somewhat tougher questions in a dozen categories with no alphabetical clues. No specific scoring guidelines, but half right isn't bad. The categories are:

Political Parties
Foreign Words
Astronomy
Literary Characters
Mythology
Anatomy
The Dance
Sea Creatures
Art
Music
Architecture
Countries of the World

Political Parties and Their Candidates

Name the political parties representing these presidential candidates on
the dates shown.

1. 1948–J. Strom Thurmond
2. 1832–William Wirt
3. 1860–John Bell
4. 1904–Eugene V. Debs
5. 1792–Thomas Jefferson
6. 1972–John G. Schmitz
7. 1908–William J. Bryan
8. 1840–William Harrison
9. 1876–Peter Cooper
10. 1992–Ross Perot
11. 1856–John C. Frémont
12. 1888–Clinton B. Fisk
13. 1912–Theodore Roosevelt
14. 1864–Abraham Lincoln
15. 1812–DeWitt Clinton

Foreign Words

The three foreign words that constitute each question have the same
English meaning. Spellings are phonetic. What is the word in English?

1. Arzt (German), vrach (Russian), lekarz (Polish)
2. groda (Swedish), rana (Italian), grenouille (French)
3. guerra (Portuguese), ourlog (Dutch), krig (Danish)
4. chanzir (Arabic), buta (Japanese), porc (Rumanian)
5. dinero (Spanish), raha (Finnish), argent (French)
6. etsba (Hebrew), vinger (Dutch), dito (Italian)
7. fluture (Rumanian), lepke (Hungarian), mariposa (Spanish)
8. Liebe (German), ai (Japanese), amore (Italian)
9. potage (French), sopa (Spanish), minestra (Italian)
10. tomato (Japanese), pomidor (Polish), tamatim (Arabic)
11. cero (Spanish), noll (Swedish), nulla (Hungarian)
12. zub (Czech), fog (Hungarian), dent (French)
13. haut (French), alto (Italian), hoch (German)
14. sukari (Swahili), sukker (Norwegian), Zucker (German)
15. perc (Hungarian), fun (Japanese), minuto (Portuguese)

Astronomy

1. Nearest celestial object; the only natural satellite of the earth.

2. Polish astronomer who disputed the idea that the earth was the center of the universe and postulated that the sun was the center.

3. Another name for the constellation known as the Big Bear or Ursa Major.

4. This planet has a hot liquid core.

5. Largest planet in the solar system, with a mean diameter of about 88,000 miles.

6. The earth, moon, sun, stars, and planets collectively are known as the visible ____.

7. Julius Caesar and Pope Gregory XIII introduced corrections of this time-recording table.

8. The rotation of the earth is the basis for the measurement of ____.

9. Andromeda and the Milky Way are ____.

10. In addition to the large, well-known planets, there are very small planets known as ____.

11. In 1986 British scientists discovered a hole in the heavens in what is called the ____.

12. A very small star, often shrunken from a larger one, and midway in size between a white dwarf and a black hole, is called a ____.

Literary Characters

1. In what book by what author does Mr. Bumble appear?

2. Rip Van Winkle is a character in the book ____ by ____.

3. A beautiful gypsy dancer is a character in *Notre Dame de Paris* by Victor Hugo. Name her.

4. Name the hero of John Bunyan's *Pilgrim's Progress* who flees from the City of Destiny to the Celestial City.

5. In Cervantes's novel, *Don Quixote*, who is Quixote's companion who quotes proverbs and rides an ass?

6. Gargantua is the hero in a romantic novel of the same name. Name the author.

7. The "lily maid of Astolat" in Tennyson's *Idylls of the King* is ____.

8. Heroine of Thackeray's *Vanity Fair*.

9. Who wrote *Jane Eyre*?

10. Kipling wrote a tale about an orphan child in India. What is that child's name?

11. Charles Kingsley titled a novel with the name of a beautiful woman from Alexandria, later murdered. Who is she?

12. In what novel does Jean Valjean appear, and who was the author?

Mythology

1. Son of Titans, condemned to carry the heavens on his shoulders.
2. Greek goddess of the dawn, sister of the sun and moon.
3. Winged horse which rose from the blood of Medusa.
4. Founder of Corinth, condemned to hell for his crimes, where he had to spend eternity rolling a stone to the top of a steep hill only to have it roll down again.
5. The muse of poetry.
6. God of goatherds and their flocks, a shaggy half-human with goat's horns, legs, and pointed ears.
7. River that flows around Hades.
8. Greek mountain nymph whose love for Narcissus was not returned. She pined away until only her voice was left.
9. Youth loved by Aphrodite. He died after being injured by a boar.
10. God of gates and doors, represented with a double-faced head.
11. Beautiful shepherd boy loved by the moon-goddess Helene.
12. Mythical animal in ancient Greek art, half horse, half griffin.

Anatomy

1. This part of the body contains these bones: frontal, parietal, temporal, and occipital.

2. Hiccups are caused by spastic contractions of the ____.

3. The esophagus and pharynx are part of the ____.

4. The term *external nares* refers to the ____.

5. Name a fluid in the bloodstream similar to blood but without the red corpuscles.

6. The retina is the inner part of the eyeball. The middle part is the choroid. What is the outer part called?

7. About 4 percent of body weight is attributed to this organ.

8. What is the white half-moon at the base of a fingernail called?

9. The muscle which forms the upper part of the arm at the shoulders is the ____.

10. In what part of the body is the metatarsal bone found?

11. The connective tissues that bind the bones together are called the ____.

12. The main artery is the ____.

The Dance

1. Lively dance in $3/4$ time with stamping and heel clicking; the national dance of Poland. It was popular in Europe in the 1800s.

2. A native Hawaiian dance that offended missionaries because of its sensuous movements.

3. This folk dance—a whirling, flirtatious dance done with tambourines and castanets—originated in southern Italy.

4. Argentine ballroom dance.

5. Round dance resembling a slowed-down polka.

6. 1920s ballroom dance in which dancers kick sideways with one foot and simultaneously pivot with the other.

7. Graceful dance from the French that became the favorite dance at the court of Louis XIV. Mozart and Hayden composed music for it.

8. Jazz dance popular in the 1920s, with much shaking of the body.

9. Native dance of Martinique, similar to the rumba.

10. Acrobatic dance, usually performed by a single couple.

11. Theatrical dance originating in Italian courts, a favorite of Catherine de Médicis.

12. Solo dance with complicated footwork, often danced to the music of a wooden pipe.

Sea Creatures

1. Small fish of the genus Hippocampus. The largest of these are only about 5 inches long.

2. Large member of the order Cetacea, possessing a sort of sonar called echolocation.

3. Large mammal found in tropical waters of the Indian and Western Pacific oceans, belonging to the same order as the manatee.

4. Big sea mammal with tusks, found in .both the Atlantic and Pacific oceans.

5. Marine mollusk that adheres to stones or other objects in shallow water, of which many species are used for food.

6. Some of these fish are harmless, but others, like the great white, attack humans.

7. Blue jellyfish with poisonous tentacles.

8. These marine animals have seal-like flippers. They come ashore only to lay eggs.

9. Aquatic carnivore related to the weasel. These animals live in dens with underwater entrances.

10. Small ocean fish tightly packed in cans for food.

11. Simple animal with no vertebrae. Their species dates back 600 million years.

12. Also called the rosefish, this commercial food fish is found in temperate waters of the Atlantic Ocean.

Art

1. American artist known for his seascapes, such as *The Fog Warning*.

2. This farmer's wife took up painting when she was past 70.

3. What is the term used for a sculpture in which the figures are raised from the background?

4. Name the Swiss painter who painted *Twittering Machine*.

5. Sir Joshua Reynolds painted a famous portrait of an innocent child. What is the title of that portrait?

6. The goddess of dawn was painted on the ceiling of a garden house at a Roman palace in 1609. What is the title of the painting and who was the artist?

7. Paintings which give the illusion of reality are termed ____.

8. Give the title of Leonardo Da Vinci's painting of the twelve Apostles.

9. Pop artist, also a filmmaker.

10. A well-known portrait of George Washington hangs in the Museum of Fine Arts, Boston. Name the painter.

11. Who painted *Aristotle Contemplating the Bust of Homer*?

12. What artist created the statue *The End of the Trail*, depicting a dejected and weary Indian warrior sitting on a pony?

Music

1. Composer of *The Blue Danube*.
2. He wrote the piece popularly known as *The Song of India*.
3. Drums, triangles, and chimes are examples of ___ instruments.
4. Who wrote the oratorio *The Messiah*?
5. Piano virtuoso, creator of *Prometheus*.
6. He composed classic American folk songs, as *O, Susanna*.
7. A notation that represents two whole notes or four half notes.
8. Name given to a vocal solo from opera or oratorio accompanied by orchestral music.
9. Brass instrument created by Adolphe Sax, using a single reed.
10. First symphony orchestra in the U.S., founded in 1842.
11. "Evening music" is called a ___.
12. A concluding musical section played at the end of a composition that is distinct from the main piece is called a ___.

Architecture

1. Where is the palace of King Minos?

2. This beautiful Gothic cathedral is located near Paris.

3. Architect famed for his outstanding works, such as Roble House in Chicago.

4. Creator of the "geodesic dome" concept. It is said that he does not consider himself an architect.

5. Contemporary building in New York City designed by Eero Saarinen.

6. The semicircular area in a church, usually containing the altar, is called the ____.

7. Architect of St. Paul's Cathedral, London.

8. Ceremonial burial vaults for Egyptian pharaohs; one of the Seven Wonders of the ancient world.

9. Roman building of antiquity for which the only source of light is an opening at the top of the dome.

10. Reconstructed medieval building moved from various European sites to New York City; part of the Metropolitan Museum of Art.

11. This American writer's home at Cambridge, Massachusetts, is an example of colonial architecture.

12. The Pan Am building in Manhattan was designed by ____.

Countries of the World

1. The capital of this Muslim republic is Dhaka. The official language is Bengali.

2. This land of the Bantu in central Africa was probably inhabited by the Pygmies in its early history.

3. Languages spoken here include German, French, Italian, and Romansh. Watch and clock-making are important industries.

4. It occupies over 70 percent of the Arabian peninsula. Dates are exported. There is no rain from June to December.

5. This commonwealth occupies almost 3 million square miles. It is divided into 6 states.

6. This "république" is bounded on the north by the English Channel.

7. This kingdom's national anthem is the "Marche Real." The river Ebro is here.

8. This state was established in 1948. Its parliament is called the Knesset.

9. Grand duchy in Europe, smaller than Rhode Island, with a 100 percent literacy rate.

10. Its capital is Doha. It's an oil-producing country with a largely Muslim population.

11. South American country. Currency is the inti; coins include soles and sols. All education is free.

12. Most residents are Lutheran in this northern European republic. The markka is the unit of currency.

Answers to
Section I

A Answers

1. ANASTASIA
2. ALBATROSS
3. ABELARD
4. ALHAMBRA
5. ANDROID
6. ANSEL ADAMS
7. ASTA
8. ACOUSTICS
9. ABACUS
10. AMBROSIA
11. APPLE
12. ALLITERATION
13. ALLAH
14. ALGORISM
15. ARTICHOKE
16. ATTILA
17. ACK-ACK
18. ALBINO
19. AMATI
20. APES
21. ARGONAUTS
22. ASPEN
23. ANDERSONVILLE
24. ALGEBRA
25. AFRIKAANS
26. ATLANTIS
27. ASPIDISTRA

28. ALCATRAZ
29. ASPARTAME
30. ANTIBODIES
31. ALCHEMISTS
32. ALFRED ADLER
33. AVANT-GARDE
34. ASTRAKHAN
35. ATLANTA
36. ARMADILLO
37. AQUARIUS
38. ADAM'S APPLE
39. ANOREXIA
40. APERITIF
41. ARPEGGIO
42. ARTHUR ASHE
43. ABIGAIL ADAMS, wife of President John Adams.
44. ALASKA. The state has proven rich in natural resources.
45. AMETHYST
46. THE ALAMO
47. ALUMINUM
48. ARARAT
49. ACUPUNCTURE. There are 800 designated points. In the U.S. acupuncture is usually done only on an experimental basis.
50. AYATOLLAH

B Answers

1. BULL
2. BROOKLYN
3. BIGFOOT
4. BAGPIPE
5. BATS
6. BETA BLOCKER
7. BRENDAN BEHAN
8. BOWIE KNIFE
9. THE BIG BANG
10. BANGLADESH
11. BEETHOVEN
12. BASENJI
13. BACCARAT
14. BOGEY
15. BIRD BRAIN
16. BENEDICTINE
17. BARBERSHOP
18. BRONTOSAURUS
19. BOMBE
20. BEAU BRUMMEL: His full name was George Bryan Brummel.
21. *BLUE BOY*. The original hangs in the Huntington Art Gallery in San Marino, California.
22. DR. BRUCE BANNER
23. BIG BERTHA
24. BONES
25. BUNSEN BURNER

26. BLACK BOTTOM
27. BISMARCK
28. BIG BEN
29. THE BOWERY
30. BUTTONHOOK
31. BURT BACHARACH
32. BEAUFORT. The scale is numbered; Beaufort 0 is calm, Beaufort 6 is a strong breeze, Beaufort 17 is a hurricane.
33. BLACKOUT
34. BARRISTER
35. BEN-GURION. His real name was David Green, but he thought his pen name more interesting and came to be known by it.
36. THE BEATLES
37. THE BROOKLYN BRIDGE
38. BUSH BABY
39. BRAINWASHING
40. BAKKE, ALAN
41. *THE BOUNTY*
42. BEDLOE'S ISLAND
43. BLOOMERS; named after another reformer, a Mrs. Bloomer.
44. *BEOWULF*
45. BRAILLE; Louis Braille was himself blind.
46. BUFFALO BILL. The name was allegedly given him because he shot over 4,000 buffalo during a short period of time to help feed workers who were building a railroad.
47. BIKINI
48. BARKIS
49. "BEGIN THE BEGUINE"
50. BASTILLE

C Answers

1. CLOUDS. Clouds are classified according to appearance, altitude, or composition.
2. CARLSBAD CAVERNS
3. CHARLIE CHAPLIN
4. CALLIGRAPHY
5. CLOISONNÉ
6. CORSET
7. CAKE
8. CAPE COD
9. CHESHIRE CAT
10. CARILLON
11. CAPYBARA
12. CRIBBAGE: 15 2, 15 4, and a pair is 6 is a scoring count.
13. COMET and CUPID
14. CASANOVA
15. CALLIOPE
16. CADUCEUS: A staff with two entwined snakes and two wings at the top.
17. CAPTAIN COOK
18. CALUMET
19. COLUMBO
20. CENT
21. CANINE
22. CENTILLION
23. CHAMELEON
24. CONSTANTINOPLE, the largest city in Turkey, with a population of almost 4 million.

25. CHECKERS
26. *CONSTITUTION*. She did battle with the British three times in the War of 1812 and was victorious each time.
27. CASSIUS CLAY
28. CAVIAR
29. CANTERBURY
30. CERBERUS
31. CYCLOPS
32. CLAUSTROPHOBIA
33. CONTINENTAL CONGRESS
34. CALORIE
35. CHRISTOPHER COLUMBUS
36. *CASABLANCA*
37. CHAMBER MUSIC
38. CAT SCAN
39. CONDOR, with wingspans of nine to ten feet. The condor is an endangered species.
40. THE COMSTOCK LODE. A man named Henry Comstock claimed the lode, although it was discovered by others who died before they could record their claim.
41. CIVILIAN CONSERVATION CORPS
42. CAROL CHANNING
43. CONGLOMERATE
44. CAMELOT
45. CALYPSO
46. CLYDESDALE
47. CHARLIE CHAN
48. CUBA
49. CHICHEN-ITZA
50. COLLEGE OF CARDINALS

D Answers

1. DIDEROT, DENIS
2. DUST JACKET
3. DYSLEXIA
4. DIGIT
5. DIAMOND
6. DAVID DOYLE
7. DEWEY DECIMAL SYSTEM
8. DOLPHIN. The dolphin is friendly to man and appears to have a complex language.
9. DACHSHUND
10. DUNGEONS AND DRAGONS
11. DANIEL DEFOE
12. DUVALIER, FRANÇOIS. When he died in 1971, his son Jean-Claude, Baby Doc, became President. Papa Doc is said to have practiced voodoo.
13. *THE DECAMERON*
14. DINGO
15. DOROTHY DIX
16. DORMOUSE
17. DIONNE QUINTUPLETS
18. DR. DOOLITTLE
19. DE SOTO
20. DUMBO
21. DANDELION
22. DELPHI. Messages supposedly originating with the oracle were spoken by a priestess in a trance.
23. DECIBEL. The loudest sound that the human ear can tolerate is about 120dB.

24. DESIGNERS
25. DODO
26. DIE
27. DOWSER
28. DOVE
29. DOGHOUSE
30. DEBUG
31. DEFARGE. She enjoyed watching the activity at the guillotine.
32. DÉTENTE
33. DUODECIMAL. The numbers run from 0 through 9 and then X and E. Using that number line—0 1 2 3 4 5 6 7 8 9 X E—you can see that 8 plus 2 would equal X.
34. DRACULA
35. DOVER, Delaware
36. DRUIDS. According to legend, they sacrificed human victims.
37. DNA, DEOXYRIBONUCLEIC ACID
38. DECATHLON
39. DOLDRUMS
40. DAMON
41. DAGUERREOTYPE, invented by Louis Daguerre.
42. DRONE
43. DONNER PASS. Half the party eventually reached California.
44. DOUGHBOY
45. DROMEDARY
46. DOCTOR OF DIVINITY
47. DUSTBIN
48. DUTCH DOOR
49. DENMARK
50. DÜRER, Albrecht

E Answers

1. EDDY, Mary Baker. She became interested in faith healing around 1862. She founded the *Christian Science Monitor*, which is still being published, in 1908.

2. EMU. It stands five to six feet tall and is a swift runner.

3. EQUUS

4. ELBA

5. EEG or Electroencephalograph

6. EMPRESS EUGÉNIE

7. ELECTRIC EEL

8. ENTEBBE

9. *EAST OF EDEN*

10. EXPONENT

11. EDELWEISS

12. ESPERANTO

13. THE EVERGLADES

14. ESKIMO

15. EXISTENTIALISM

16. ESP, extrasensory perception

17. EASTER ISLAND. It was discovered on Easter Sunday in 1722.

18. EMMETT, ROBERT

19. ELECTIONS

20. EQUINOX

21. EYE

22. EXCALIBUR. Arthur was able to pry the magic sword loose from an enchanted stone, although others had tried and failed. Because of this feat he was proclaimed king.

23. ECHO

24. *THE EXORCIST*
25. EDINBURGH
26. EVE
27. ELF: Extremely low frequency.
28. ENERGY. His theory of relativity postulated a constant velocity for light (c), and the equivalence of mass (m) and energy (E).
29. EPIGRAM
30. ENTREPRENEUR
31. ESTUARY
32. The EIFFEL TOWER, named after its builder, Alexandre Eiffel.
33. EUPHRATES
34. EARHART, Amelia
35. EVOLUTION
36. EMMYS
37. ERMINE
38. ELEGY (Written in a Country Church-yard).
39. EVEREST. It was not climbed until 1953, although many attempts were made prior to that date. It is over 29,000 feet high.
40. ENTOMOLOGY
41. ECTOPLASM
42. EURODOLLARS
43. EDAM
44. EQUATOR
45. EUREKA! EUREKA! The Greek mathematician discovered the displacement-of-water theory while stepping into a public bath and became so excited that he ran home without putting on his clothes. According to Tom Burnam, author of *The Dictionary of Misinformation*, this was not unusual since Greeks customarily exercised in the nude.
46. EXPLORER I
47. EDERLE, Gertrude. She did it in 14 hours and 31 minutes, beating the world record by just one minute short of two hours.
48. EUCALYPTUS
49. ESCALATOR. (Did you guess ELEVATOR? No, the first operating elevator was installed in a New York City building by Otis.)
50. EAR. The bull's ear is customarily given to a celebrity or honored guest in the audience.

F Answers

1. FANLIGHT
2. FANZINE (fan magazine)
3. FOCUS (AF = Automatic Focus)
4. FENCE
5. FLAMENCO
6. FERDINAND FOCH
7. FENCING
8. FOREST FIRES
9. FANFARE
10. *FAUST*
11. FLORA and FAUNA
12. *FRANKENSTEIN*
13. FALLOUT
14. FLEUR-DE-LIS
15. THE FORTY-NINERS
16. FRIAR
17. FLANDERS FIELD. The quotation is from the poem by John McCrae. The former country of Flanders (today, part of France, Belgium, and the Netherlands) was occupied by Germany in World War II.
18. FOKKER
19. FRIEDMAN. They are better known as Ann Landers and Abby Van Buren.
20. THE FALKLAND ISLANDS. The inhabitants are primarily of British, not Argentine, descent.
21. FANNIE FARMER
22. FINLAND

23. FORTRAN. You may have figured that out from FORmula TRANslation.

24. FIFTY-FOUR FORTY OR FIGHT. The U.S. argued that the latitude 54° 40' N. was the boundary of U.S. territories.

25. FAHRENHEIT

26. FAMILIAR

27. THE FOUR FREEDOMS: Freedom of speech, freedom of worship, freedom from want, and freedom from fear.

28. FIDDLED. Actually he was playing a lyre, according to some historians.

29. FORD, GERALD

30. FITCH, John. It was 17 years before Fulton's boat, the *Clermont*, made a successful run from New York City to Albany.

31. FEMME FATALE

32. FLAG DAY, the anniversary of the adoption of the Stars and Stripes in 1877.

33. FRANC

34. FELIX FRANKFURTER

35. FELIX the Cat

36. FUGIT. Tempus fugit means "time flies."

37. FOX-TROT

38. FLOTSAM

39. FLIBBERTIGIBBET

40. FRENCH FRIES

41. FEATHERBEDDING

42. FALSETTO

43. FRIENDS; members of the Society of Friends, a religious denomination to which William Penn belonged.

44. FISHING. His book *The Compleat Angler*, written in 1653, is one of the most famous books in English.

45. FEZ. It is still worn in some areas.

46. FONDUE

47. FRIGATE

48. The FIRTH OF FORTH. A firth is a long narrow indentation of the seacoast, and "Forth" refers to the Forth River.

49. FLAMINGO

50. FIREFLY. One variety found in Paraguay is called the railway beetle because it flashes red and green lights.

G Answers

1. GREENWICH, in England.
2. The GODFATHER. Brando won an Oscar for the role.
3. GLASSES
4. GRAFFITI
5. GREENBACKS
6. GUILLOTINE. It was last used in France in 1971.
7. GREENLAND
8. GOLDEN GATE. The main span is 4,200 feet and total length is 9,266 feet.
9. GIBSON GIRL
10. GOBI
11. GERMAINE GREER
12. GRACIAS
13. GREELEY, HORACE, an American newspaper editor who founded the *New York Tribune*.
14. GREER GARSON. The film won seven Academy Awards.
15. GUERNSEY
16. GRIFFIN
17. GIANTS
18. GUPPY
19. GUADALCANAL
20. GAUGUIN. His work, *By the Sea*, hangs in the National Gallery of Art in Washington, D.C.
21. GUMBO
22. GRETNA GREEN. It was popular then because the only requirement was a statement before witnesses that they wanted to be married.
23. GRAPHITE, a soft black carbon also used as a lubricant.

24. GROUNDHOG. If he sees his shadow he goes back into hibernation.

25. GRINCH

26. GIRL GUIDES. The next year, 1913, the name was changed to Girl Scouts.

27. GIBRALTAR

28. GEORGE GALLUP. His polls were based on disciplined sampling methods. Gallup died in 1984.

29. GABRIEL. He is also named in the Koran and the Talmud.

30. GETTYSBURG

31. GNU

32. GEORGE GERSHWIN

33. GREGG; both Pitman and Gregg are shorthand systems.

34. GAELIC, although everyone speaks English. Gaelic is a Celtic language.

35. GIRAFFE

36. GROMYKO

37. GOLD DIGGER

38. GRIMM, Jacob and Wilhelm, known as the Brothers Grimm.

39. GERBIL

40. GENE

41. GAMMA GLOBULIN

42. GALAXY

43. GYPSUM, a soft mineral

44. GOURD. It bears fruit in odd shapes with hard shells.

45. GUATEMALA

46. *The GREAT GATSBY*

47. GREGORY XIII. He ordered ten days to be stricken from the calendar to bring it more into conformity with reality.

48. GYMNASIUM

49. GERONIMO

50. GALILEO, considered a heretic by the Church because he believed in a solar system with the earth revolving around the sun.

H Answers

1. HARPSICHORD
2. HIPPOCRATES. The Hippocratic Oath is the basis of the code of ethics of the medical profession.
3. HELIUM
4. HUMAN
5. HOVERCRAFT
6. HOCKEY (FIELD)
7. HAIKU
8. HARP. The other side of each coin portrays an animal.
9. HELSINKI
10. HARRY HOUDINI
11. HUSKY
12. HUBERT HORATIUS HUMPHREY
13. HAMSTRINGS
14. HORNBOOK. It was in use until the mid-eighteenth century by children learning to read.
15. HELEN HAYES
16. HAGGIS
17. HAWAII. The volcano is double-cratered.
18. HEDDA HOPPER
19. HARVARD. It was founded with a grant from the Massachusetts Bay Colony.
20. The HERMITAGE
21. The HEIMLICH maneuver, in which one exerts pressure to expel the object that is caught in the throat.
22. HANDLE
23. HEMLOCK

24. HEALTH
25. HERCULES
26. HICCUP
27. HIROHITO
28. HAYSEED
29. HOMER
30. HERALDRY
31. HIAWATHA. The name means "he makes rivers."
32. HANGOVER
33. HAVANA, CUBA
34. HOMEOPATHY
35. HIGHBROW
36. HUMPERDINCK, ENGELBERT
37. HOYLE. Although Edmund Hoyle died in 1769, his name is still associated with rules for playing cards.
38. THE HEADLESS HORSEMAN
39. HEMOPHILIA
40. HITCHCOCK
41. THE HAGUE
42. HAM
43. HAMMER. The hammer and sickle is the emblem of the Soviet Union and appears on its flag.
44. HURON, the fifth largest lake in the world.
45. HYPOCHONDRIAC
46. HEXAGON
47. HIEROGLYPHICS
48. HARPOON
49. HOLOGRAM
50. HANUKKAH. It is marked by the lighting of candles in an eight-branched candelabrum called a menorah.

I Answers

1. IRELAND
2. IVORY
3. INSTITUTION. A common error is to refer to it as the Smithsonian Institute.
4. ILLUSIONS
5. INFINITY
6. IBIS, often portrayed in Egyptian paintings and sculptures.
7. ISABELLA I
8. IDENTIKIT
9. IMPRESSIONIST, a way of painting favored by, among others, Renoir, Monet, Pissaro, and Degas.
10. ICBM, intercontinental ballistic missile (supersonic).
11. IOTA
12. ISOSCELES
13. IMPASSE
14. INCANDESCENT
15. ICARUS
16. INFERNO
17. INVERTEBRATE
18. ISIS, the nature goddess.
19. I.O.U.
20. An ICEBERG
21. The INDIANAPOLIS (INDY) 500
22. IT. The word comes from a 1927 novel by Eleanor Glyn.
23. IMPRESARIO
24. INDONESIA
25. IAMBIC. An iamb is a metrical foot consisting of one short

syllable followed by a long one, or one unstressed syllable followed by one stressed syllable.

26. ISLAM
27. IMPEACHMENT. The impeachment was a political maneuver by Johnson's opponents. Republicans induced the House of Representatives to impeach Johnson before the Senate as a high court, and only by a narrow margin did he escape expulsion from the Presidency.
28. INDIA INK
29. INTERPOL, which comes from the organization's name, International Criminal Police Organization. More than 100 countries are members.
30. IODINE
31. *THE ILIAD*
32. I.W.W., Industrial Workers of the World, a once-powerful militant labor union.
33. INSULIN. A deficiency of this hormone leads to diabetes.
34. IMHOTEP. He was worshipped as a god after his death.
35. The IROQUOIS LEAGUE. The Five Nations were Mohawk, Oneida, Onondaga, Cayuga, and Seneca.
36. INDEPENDENCE, Missouri, where he and wife Bess had their home.
37. IRIS
38. IDES
39. I.Q. (intelligence quotient).
40. IRON Curtain
41. INTERMEZZO
42. IGUANA
43. ILLUMINATED
44. "IRONSIDE"
45. ID, so defined by Freud.
46. IONOSPHERE. It begins at an altitude of about 30 miles and contains the electrically-charged particles by which radio waves are transmitted.
47. INVERNESS
48. INCA
49. *IVANHOE*
50. ICELAND

J K Answers

1. KIWI
2. JAZZ
3. JAMES JOYCE
4. KEN KESEY
5. JAMBALAYA
6. JAMESTOWN, VIRGINIA
7. KILIMANJARO
8. The JURASSIC period was about 180-135 million years ago, when dinosaurs roamed.
9. KAMIKAZE. They downed about 40 U.S. ships.
10. KRIS KRISTOFFERSON
11. JAGUAR, a beast about 7 feet long.
12. JOSS
13. KANGAROO, found in Australia and neighboring islands.
14. *The KATZENJAMMER KIDS*
15. The KORAN. It's the earliest known work in Arabic prose.
16. KINGSTON, a favorite tourist spot.
17. JUDO
18. KICKAPOO
19. JESSE JAMES
20. *KRAMER VS. KRAMER*
21. KETTLEDRUM
22. KATMANDU, founded in 723.
23. The KLONDIKE
24. KERMIT
25. KNOTS
26. KU KLUX KLAN

27. JEZEBEL
28. JESSE JACKSON
29. "JABBERWOCKY," from Lewis Carroll's *Through the Looking Glass*.
30. KGB, the Soviet secret police.
31. JEEP
32. JOEY
33. KIBITZ
34. KLEPTOMANIA. Although psychiatrists consider this a disease, it is not legally accepted as a defense for theft.
35. JUMBO JET
36. KUMQUAT
37. KAYAK
38. KALEIDOSCOPE
39. KUDOS
40. JARVIK 7
41. JEEVES
42. KARMA
43. KAFFEEKLATSCH
44. KRUGERRAND
45. JOHN JAKES
46. KRYPTON
47. KEWPIE
48. KUBLAI KHAN
49. KING KONG
50. JOYSTICK

L Answers

1. LORETTA LYNN
2. LOSS LEADER
3. Excerpt from old song of unknown origin, "Loch Lomond."
4. Brits call trucks "LORRIES."
5. LATCHKEY CHILDREN
6. LYCANTHROPE
7. LADYBIRD
8. LOUNGE LIZARDS
9. LOVE
10. LANOLIN
11. The LOUVRE. The Venus de Milo sculpture is here.
12. LILY LANGTRY. She was nicknamed "The Jersey Lily" because she was born in Jersey in the Channel Islands.
13. LADY LIBERTY (the Statue of Liberty).
14. LAETRILE. Its use is not generally approved by physicians.
15. LOUPE
16. *LAMPOON*. It prints original material by undergraduates.
17. LASER. The name is an acronym.
18. The *LUSITANIA*, torpedoed with no warning.
19. LEND LEASE
20. DR. LIVINGSTON. While David Livingston, a noted explorer, was exploring around Lake Tanganyika, nothing was heard from him for months and international fears for his safety arose. He was located by a rescue team headed by Dr. Henry Morton Stanley, a journalist, who is said to have commented, "Dr. Livingston, I presume."
21. LEMMINGS. It is believed they become overpopulated and, in their search for food, migrate to the sea where many, purely by accident, drown.

22. LEEK
23. LEECH
24. LISBON
25. LEPRECHAUN
26. LOOFAH
27. LOIS LANE
28. LUCKY LINDY
29. LAKE LUCERNE
30. LANDLUBBER
31. The LUFTWAFFE. The name means "air weapon."
32. LOURDES
33. LIBEL. If it is true, it is not libel; if it is spoken it is slander.
34. LAZARUS
35. LYRE
36. LIPPIZANER. Its name comes from Lipizza, Austria, where the breed was developed.
37. LORELEI
38. LLOYDS OF LONDON
39. LIMERICK
40. The letter L represents the number 50.
41. LIGHT-YEAR
42. LAISSEZ-FAIRE
43. LAND, Edwin
44. LEGERDEMAIN
45. LOBOTOMY. In this operation the frontal lobes are separated from the rest of the brain. It is rarely used today because after surgery, patients become detached and inactive.
46. LITTLE LEAGUE
47. LETTERPRESS
48. LOHENGRIN
49. LIRA
50. *LOVE'S LABOURS LOST*

M Answers

1. MUGWUMPS. The name is of Indian derivation.
2. MARIA MONTESSORI
3. *The MARATHON MAN*
4. MORAL MAJORITY. The term is also used as nomenclature for the entire religious community called the "new right."
5. MANGO
6. MENSA. To get in, you must pass a test to prove you rank in the top three percent of the population (IQ level).
7. MAGNESIUM. Like aluminum, it is not magnetic.
8. The MOLLY MAGUIRES. They fought poor working conditions and went on strike, but Pinkerton detectives broke up the organization and twenty members were hanged.
9. METHUSELAH
10. The beginning of the MIRANDA warning, telling arrested persons of their rights. The name stems from a U.S. Supreme Court case, *Miranda* v. *Arizona*, where the Court ruled as inadmissible incriminating statements taken from the accused without his being informed as to his rights.
11. The MONTGOLFIERS, Joseph-Michel and Jacques-Étienne.
12. MARZIPAN
13. MINUTEMEN
14. MOONIE, after its founder Sun Myung Moon, a Korean evangelist.
15. MARSHALL MCLUHAN. He had unorthodox views on communication, and the quotation means that the means by which a message is communicated may influence people more than the message itself.

16. MIL. The strength of plastic trash bags is ordinarily measured in mils.

17. MORTARBOARD

18. MARGARET MEAD

19. A MOLE

20. The MUPPETS

21. MANTRA

22. MAURICE MAETERLINCK. He was awarded the Nobel Prize in literature in 1911.

23. MONOPOLY

24. MITTERAND, François

25. MONDRIAN, Piet. His paintings were made with rectangles and were in primary colors and white and black.

26. MANTILLA

27. MIDAS. He asked the gods to grant him the power to make everything he touched turn to gold. But when he touched food, that also turned to gold, and he asked the gods to take back their gift.

28. MANX

29. MODEM

30. The MAGI: Melchior, Caspar, and Balthazar.

31. The MOA. It could not fly.

32. The MAFIA, also known as Cosa Nostra.

33. MING. Beautiful bronze, porcelain, and lacquered pieces were created during this time. The dynasty ruled China between 1368 and 1644.

34. MAH-JONGG. The name was coined by Joseph Babcock, who brought the game to America.

35. The MORMONS. The proper name is Church of Jesus Christ of Latter-day Saints.

36. MAID MARIAN

37. MONGOOSE

38. Prof. MORIARITY

39. MACH NUMBER, named after its inventor, Ernst Mach. If a plane flies at Mach 2, it is traveling twice as fast as the speed of sound.

40. THE MUNCHKINS

41. MARABEL MORGAN. In her book she advises women to be submissive.
42. MULE
43. MORSE code
44. MICKEY MANTLE
45. MALTHUS
46. MADAME
47. The MULE
48. MOTOWN
49. MICHELANGELO
50. MISS MARPLE

N Answers

1. NOCTURNE
2. NECTARINE
3. NOVA. The star may become a million times more luminous for a short time.
4. NEEDLEPOINT
5. NISEI
6. NEWCASTLE. The saying means it is foolish to do something superfluous, Newcastle, England, being a coal-producing country.
7. NUMISMATIST. The term is also used for those who collect medals, tokens, and paper money.
8. NESSIE
9. NEGOTIABLE. NOW stands for Negotiable Order of Withdrawal.
10. NARC or NARCO
11. NEPOTISM
12. NEWPORT NEWS
13. NAIROBI
14. *NAUTILUS*. It was named after the underwater ship in Jules Verne's *20,000 Leagues Under the Sea*.
15. NARCISSUS. He was turned into a flower by the gods as a rebuke for his excessive vanity.
16. NUREMBERG, Germany
17. NYET
18. "NEVERMORE"
19. NOVELLA
20. NIPPON
21. NEO-NAZI
22. NAZARETH

23. NATO, North Atlantic Treaty Organization.
24. NADIR
25. NIMBUS
26. NERVOUS NELLY
27. NOBEL, ALFRED
28. NEBUCHADNEZZAR II
29. NIHILISM
30. THE NEANDERTHAL MAN. The place near Dusseldorf was Neanderthal.
31. NOME
32. NASHVILLE
33. The *NUTCRACKER Suite*
34. NITROGLYCERIN
35. NETWORKING
36. NOSTRADAMUS
37. NEUFCHÂTEL
38. NECTAR
39. NYLON
40. NEWSPEAK
41. NAZIMOVA. When her director met with censorship in Russia, he and Nazimova moved to Berlin, where the play was presented, followed by production in London and New York, all in 1905.
42. NICKELODEON. The name was later adopted for the five-cent jukebox.
43. NIGHTINGALE
44. NAPOLEON
45. NITPICKING
46. NEOMYCIN
47. NAGASAKI
48. NEMESIS. This is also the name given to the "death star" by scientists who believe that periodic mass extinctions of life on our planet are caused by showers of comets from this star as it hits the earth. But don't worry, the next extinction is not due for several million years.
49. NEFERTITI
50. NOYES, ALFRED

O Answers

1. OBELISK. Cleopatra's Needle, in New York, is 69 feet high. It was given to the U.S. in the 1800s by Egyptian rulers.
2. OPAL. The stone is believed by some to bring bad luck.
3. OBI
4. ORANGUTAN
5. OKEECHOBEE. The lake occupies 730 square miles.
6. OMBUDSMAN. The idea originated in Sweden, and the Swedish word means "legal representative."
7. OPHTHALMOLOGIST. Both an oculist and an optometrist examine eyes and prescribe glasses. An optician makes eyeglasses. Only an ophthalmologist is a medical doctor. The *ph* is pronounced *f* as in "phrase" or "phantom."
8. OLIVE OYL
9. ORIGAMI
10. OOLONG. The name means "black dragon" in Chinese.
11. OBERAMMERGAU. Every two years, village residents act out the death and resurrection of Christ, in obedience to a vow made during the plague in 1633.
12. ORNITHOLOGIST
13. OSCAR
14. OMEGA. The Greek alphabet has 24 characters, from alpha to omega.
15. OCARINA
16. OBERON
17. OCELOT. It inhabits Central and South America.
18. ONYX
19. OXFORD. The university has been a center of learning since the 12th century.

20. OREGANO
21. OZARKS
22. OYEZ
23. OSLO. It used to be called Christiania.
24. ORBIT
25. OKIE. The term is also applied to natives of Okinawa.
26. The OREGON TRAIL, about 2,000 miles long. When he set up trading posts, John Jacob Astor sent men to scout the old trail. The trip took early pioneers five or six months.
27. ORION
28. OSTRICH
29. OCTOPUS. These sea creatures can change color as they wish.
30. O'CONNOR, Sandra Day. She was sworn in in 1981 at the age of 51.
31. OPIUM. China prohibited the importation of opium from Britain. Britain won the war, and was given Hong Kong.
32. OLAV V. He was actually born in England, but was Norwegian by ancestry and citizenship.
33. OYSTERS
34. ORTHOPEDICS
35. OPTIMIST. The pessimist, of course, sees the glass as half empty.
36. OAKLEY, Annie. She was so good with a rifle that she could shoot a playing card tossed in the air, and do it several times as it was falling.
37. ONE-UPMANSHIP
38. OUIJA board
39. OXYMORON
40. ODIN. He held court in Valhalla as the god of war.
41. OXYGEN, a colorless, tasteless gas essential to life. It was discovered in 1774. Oxygen makes up 60 percent of the human body.
42. ORANGEMAN, after William III of England, the Prince of Orange.
43. OMNIVORE
44. OVERALLS
45. ORATORIO. Handel's are perhaps the best known. Oratorios are often religious in nature, and ordinarily, along with no scenery, use no costumes or action.

46. OMAN

47. The OLYMPIC GAMES. At least one of the five colors on the flag appears on every national flag in the world.

48. OKAPI

49. OASIS

50. OVAL OFFICE. There are two oval rooms in the White House, the Oval Office and the oval study in the living quarters.

PQ Answers

1. PALINDROME: A word, phrase, or sentence that reads the same backward as forward: *deed, kayak, able was I ere I saw Elba.*

2. PAPERHANGER

3. The PENTAGON

4. A PHOENIX

5. PURPLE. He wrote, "I never saw a purple cow/ I never hope to see one/ but I can tell you anyhow /I'd rather see than be one."

6. POLTERGEIST

7. PINKIE

8. PENUCHE

9. PI. 3.1416 is the ratio between the circumference of a circle and its diameter. Mathematicians have tried to carry out the fractional .1416 (actually .14159 +) to some finite number, to no avail—it stretches out forever.

10. QUICHE, a pie containing a filling such as ham or spinach. The quote is the title of a book by Bruce Feirstein.

11. PROHIBITION. Laws restricting the sale of alcoholic beverages were passed in 1919 but repealed in 1933 when citizens refused to obey them.

12. QUARTERMASTER

13. PROTOTYPE. EPCOT stands for Experimental Prototype Community of Tomorrow.

14. POKER

15. QUISLING, so called after Vidkun Quisling. He was executed for treason.

16. PBX (Private Branch Exchange)

17. PELÉ, Edson Arantes do Nascimento.

18. PALOMINO

19. POLYGRAPH

20. PASSENGER PIGEON. Officials at the Cincinnati Zoo named her Martha. The pigeons were hunted to death.

21. QUASIMODO

22. POINTILLISM

23. PELICAN. The well-known verse was written by a little-remembered author, Dixon Lanier Merritt. He wrote, "A wonderful bird is the pelican/His bill will hold more than his belican/He can take in his beak/Enough food for a week/But I'm damned if I know how the helican."

24. PACEMAKER

25. PALIMONY

26. QUEENS

27. POLITBURO. It used to be called the Presidium.

28. QUICKSILVER. It is used in thermometers because it's the only common metal that remains liquid at ordinary temperatures.

29. PHINEAS

30. PEPYS, Samuel. The words are from his diary, written in cipher in 1660. It was discovered and deciphered after his death.

31. PAGO PAGO

32. PANDAS. Ling-Ling, a female, and Hsing-Hsing, a male, were given by China to the National Zoo in Washington, D.C.

33. QUASAR. Some scientists have thought they guard the edges of the world, but nobody knows exactly what they are, except that they are star-like objects so distant that their light and radio waves take millions or billions of years to reach earth.

34. PABLO PICASSO

35. PIRANHA. It can quickly strip flesh from fish and animals.

36. QUAIL

37. QUININE, derived from the bark of the cinchona tree. The taste is markedly bitter.

38. QUARTERDECK

39. PARKS, Rosa. Her actions were the catalyst that sparked a major civil rights movement.

40. PINOCCHIO, from the book by Carlo Collodi (Carlo Lorenzini).

41. QUARTZ
42. *PEYTON PLACE*
43. PLATYPUS
44. PHILADELPHIA
45. PARTHENON, one of the world's great architectural works.
46. POSTPARTUM
47. QUADRILLE. The word also refers to paper marked in squares, as graph paper.
48. PAINE, Thomas
49. PHILLIPS
50. PEPPERMINT PATTY

R Answers

1. RASPUTIN. He was murdered by a group of nobles.
2. ROOK
3. The RIVIERA
4. Cowboy star ROY ROGERS
5. RODGERS, RICHARD. They also collaborated on *South Pacific* and *Oklahoma!*
6. RUNNYMEDE, a meadow on the bank of the Thames River, a few miles from Windsor, where the Magna Carta was signed.
7. ROUND ROBIN
8. REVEILLE
9. RENO, Nevada
10. RADAR, short for Radio Detection and Ranging
11. ROMULUS and REMUS
12. ROUGH RIDERS, mostly cowboys and ranchers, organized and commanded by Theodore Roosevelt.
13. ROBOTS, in *Star Wars* trilogy.
14. RHUBARB
15. RADIUS
16. The RORSCHACH test. Patients are asked to tell what each design suggests to them.
17. ROC. The bird was so strong and powerful that he could snatch up elephants and carry them off.
18. ROBERTS, Henry Martyn, creator of *Robert's Rules of Order.*
19. REAGAN, RONALD
20. RHOMBOID
21. REDWOOD
22. RATTLESNAKE
23. RUGBY

24. ROCHESTER, Minnesota
25. The RUBICON
26. RHODES, Cecil. He founded scholarships for 32 American students (Rhodes Scholars) each year at Oxford University.
27. RIDE, SALLY, A MISSION SPECIALIST AND FLIGHT ENGINEER IN THE 1983 SHUTTLE FLIGHT.
28. ROLLS-ROYCE
29. REINCARNATION
30. A RAINBOW
31. ROMANY
32. RUMRUNNERS
33. The ROSETTA STONE. It provided a key to deciphering Egyptian hieroglyphics.
34. ROSIE the RIVETER
35. ROADRUNNER
36. The *RUBAIYAT*. The word means "quatrains."
37. REPONDEZ. The phrase is "Repondez s'il vous plaît" (reply, please).
38. REUTERS. The agency has a German name because it was founded in Germany but moved to London in 1951.
39. RENAISSANCE
40. RICHMOND, Virginia
41. REYKJAVIK
42. RUMPELSTILTSKIN. She guesses his name and he disappears.
43. RAVIOLI
44. RX. The *R* stands for *recipe*.
45. ROBERT RIPLEY, AUTHOR OF *BELIEVE IT OR NOT*.
46. ROGER
47. ROB ROY
48. REQUIEM
49. RINGLING Brothers. They started with a little one-wagon show, later bought out Barnum and Bailey.
50. REST & RELAXATION

S Answers

1. SCRIMSHAW
2. SUMMER SOLSTICE
3. SAKI. It is usually served hot.
4. SHALOM
5. SARI. It consists of several yards of cloth draped over shoulders and arms.
6. The SEVEN SEAS
7. SCHEHEREZADE. She was wife of a sultan who decreed he would take a new wife each day. But Scheherezade would tell a story each night, saving the ending until the next night. Wanting to hear the end of each story, the sultan would spare her life until the next night. This went on for 1,001 nights, until the sultan so admired her that he revoked his decree.
8. "STARS and STRIPES." If you answered "The Star Spangled Banner," count that answer right.
9. SEABEES (C.B.; short for combat battalion).
10. SIRIUS. It is 20 times brighter than the sun and much larger than the sun, but so far away that it appears smaller and less bright.
11. S.R.O. (Standing Room Only)
12. SPUTNIK, launched by the Soviets in 1957.
13. SAMPAN
14. SIXTY-FOUR
15. SILKWORM. A silkworm can spin a cocoon from one strand of silk half a mile long.
16. STONEHENGE. It is thought that the formation was used as either a religious monument or an astronomical observatory.
17. SCORPION. Their sting is not really dangerous to humans.
18. SCUBA (Self-Contained Underwater Breathing Apparatus).
19. SKYSCRAPER

20. SULLIVAN. Sir Arthur Seymour Sullivan wrote the music and W. S. Gilbert the lyrics.

21. SALEM

22. SANSKRIT

23. SEMAPHORE

24. SOCIAL SECURITY, adopted in 1935. The first check went to a Vermont woman, in 1940, for $22.54.

25. SKULL

26. SPELEOLOGY. There is a National Speleological Society.

27. STAMPS (postage).

28. STAGECOACH

29. The SOLAR SYSTEM

30. SAIGON. It was renamed after the Vietnam War.

31. SHRDLU. ETAOIN SHRDLU are the most-used letters in the English language, in order of frequency.

32. SANDWICH, Earl of. John Montagu would not leave his card game to eat and instead would have a servant bring him this—meat between slices of bread.

33. SAM SNEAD

34. *SILENT SPRING*. This bestseller created great controversy.

35. SIRHAN SIRHAN

36. SAT (Scholastic Achievement Test)

37. SALOME

38. STANLEY CUP

39. SOLOMON

40. SCHOONER

41. SANCTUM SANCTORUM

42. STALACTITES are the "icicles" that *hang* from the roof. Those that rise up from the floor are STALAGMITES.

43. SHAKERS; more properly, members of the United Society of Believers in Christ's Second Appearing.

44. SEISMOGRAPH

45. SONNET

46. The SECRET SERVICE

47. SAWBUCK

48. The SILVER STAR

49. The SWASTIKA

50. SHILLELAGH

T Answers

1. TRANSVAAL
2. THEOSOPHY
3. TRIDENT. Another name for Neptune was POSEIDON.
4. TOUCHÉ. In popular usage, the term is an acknowledgment of repartee that hit its mark.
5. TORY
6. TARZAN
7. TREFOIL
8. TOM THUMB or GENERAL TOM THUMB, one of P. T. Barnum's performers.
9. TSUNAMI
10. TOPSY-TURVY
11. THREE
12. TWEEDLEDUM and TWEEDLEDEE
13. TAIWAN
14. TOMORROW
15. TONGUE TWISTER
16. TROY. Excavations at the site from then to 1938 uncovered villages, a fortress, a palace, and other buildings.
17. TOMMY TUCKER
18. TORAH
19. TIFFANY. The partners were Charles L. Tiffany and John B. Young.
20. TABASCO sauce
21. TOMATO. It used to be thought the tomato was poisonous.
22. TECUMSEH. He fought for the British, against the Americans, in the War of 1812.

23. The TULIP. "Tulipomania" in Holland caused people to go bankrupt due to speculation in tulip stock, and the government was compelled to intervene.
24. TOLKIEN, J. R. R., author of *The Lord of the Rings*.
25. The TSE-TSE FLY
26. The *TITANIC*. She was struck by an iceberg in the Atlantic Ocean in 1912.
27. TAROT. A tarot deck consists of picture cards of the sun, death, a hanged man, and/or other symbols. Tarot cards are used for telling fortunes.
28. TOPIARY
29. TUSKEGEE Institute
30. TRUFFLES
31. THAILAND
32. TUSSAUD'S. Marie Tussaud began modeling heads in France, while serving time in prison. She later established a wax museum in London.
33. TINY TIM. The couple were divorced.
34. THISTLE
35. TÊTE-À-TÊTE
36. TAU
37. TOM. Tom, Dick, and Harry represent ordinary people, the man in the street.
38. TOTEM pole. The figures are the totems, emblems of the person and his family.
39. TAMMANY HALL ruled the city for years, but is not politically active today.
40. TUFFET
41. TELLER, EDWARD. The hydrogen bomb is also called the thermonuclear bomb and is more powerful than the atom bomb.
42. TRUTH. The drug is popularly known as truth serum, as it leads one to talk without inhibition when questioned.
43. TGIF. Thank God It's Friday.
44. THALIDOMIDE
45. TENNIEL, Sir John. He also did political cartoons.
46. TORT

47. THATCHER, Margaret, who became P.M. in 1979.
48. The TEAMSTERS, International Brotherhood of Teamsters, Chauffeurs, Warehousemen, and Helpers of America, with over 2 million members, of whom the majority are truck drivers.
49. TINSEL TOWN, sometimes Ticky Tacky Tinsel Town.
50. TOM-TOM

U V Answers

1. ST. VALENTINE
2. VIPERS
3. URANUS. The discovery was made by accident. It takes 84 years for Uranus to make a single orbit around the sun.
4. UNMENTIONABLES
5. UNICEF. The United Nations International Children's Emergency Fund provides health care and educational services.
6. VITAMINS
7. ULSTER
8. UFO, Unidentified Flying Object.
9. VIKINGS, one of whom, Leif Eriksson, is said to have discovered North America.
10. The UNTOUCHABLES, segregated because it was thought the higher castes would be defiled by their touch. The caste system was legally ended in the 1940s.
11. ULTRASOUND, used in diagnostic medicine.
12. URANIUM
13. VATICAN CITY, in Rome.
14. VAMPIRE
15. UNITARIAN-UNIVERSALIST
16. Mount VESUVIUS, the volcano that destroyed Pompeii in the year 79, when the top of the mountain blew off.
17. VENTRICLES
18. VENI, VIDI, VICI ("I came, I saw, I conquered")
19. VERRAZANO-Narrows Bridge, a large suspension bridge.
20. UNICORN. It is depicted as pure white, symbol of holiness and chastity.

21. ULTRAVIOLET

22. VICHY. Its main industry is bottling a water carrying its name.

23. U-boat, from the German *Unterseeboot*.

24. VASSAR. The college was chartered in 1861 and named after Matthew Vassar, who donated the land and financial aid.

25. UTRILLO, Maurice

26. VACUUM, from Benedict (Baruch) Spinoza's *Ethics*: "Nature abhors a vacuum."

27. VICUÑA

28. VOUS

29. UMLAUT. It consists of two dots over a specified vowel and indicates a change in pronunciation of that vowel.

30. VOODOO

31. ULNA

32. VISCOUNT

33. URAL. The range extends about 1500 miles.

34. VANILLA

35. THULE

36. VOICEPRINT

37. VERONA, as in *Two Gentlemen of Verona*.

38. UGANDA. Swahili is widely spoken, but the official language is English.

39. VIREO

40. VOLUME; "a" being one of the edges.

41. VIOLIN

42. VERNE, Jules. He also wrote *20,000 Leagues Under the Sea* and *The MYSTERIOUS ISLAND*.

43. VIROLOGIST

44. UNSER, AL

45. VELLUM

46. VULTURE. This was your second chance; see 39–C.

47. The VOLGA, over 2,000 miles long.

48. VERMEER, Jan. Only 35 of his paintings are known to be extant.

49. The VISIGOTHS

50. VANCE, Cyrus

W X Answers

1. WENCESLAUS. The song actually refers to the duke of Bohemia who brought Christianity to his people, rather than to King Wenceslaus.

2. WINDMILLS. The phrase "tilting at windmills" has come to mean confronting imaginary enemies. Don Quixote thought windmills were giants and fought them.

3. XAVIER, St. Francis. He was canonized as a saint in 1622.

4. WATER

5. WATERSPOUT

6. WIDOW'S WALK

7. WILLIAM WORDSWORTH. He was 23 when his first poems were published.

8. WOBEGON

9. WHITE. WASP stands for White Anglo-Saxon Protestant.

10. WALLIS WARFIELD. Her first name was Bessie but she used her middle name. Edward abdicated the British throne to marry her.

11. XYLOPHONE

12. XANTHIPPE

13. WALLABY

14. XEROX. Only a copy made on a Xerox photocopier can correctly be called a Xerox copy.

15. X, as in Malcolm X.

16. WARP

17. WHISTLER. The portrait is often called *Whistler's Mother*.

18. WINDSOCK

19. *WAR OF THE WORLDS*

20. WAMPUM

21. MR. WHIPPLE

22. XL, for extra large.

23. WATERLOO, in what is now Belgium. Napoleon was exiled to the island of St. Helena following his defeat.

24. WATERGATE

25. WOODROW WILSON

26. *WHO'S WHO*

27. The WALRUS, in *Through the Looking Glass* by Lewis Carroll.

28. WATT, James, chiefly noted for his work on the steam engine.

29. WAPITI

30. WOODWIND

31. XENON

32. WILDER, Laura Ingalls

33. WEDGWOOD, named after Josiah Wedgwood, who developed the durable unglazed porcelain.

34. WIMBLEDON

35. WYNKEN, from a verse by Eugene Field. Wynken and Blynken are the two eyes, and Nod the head.

36. WOOLGATHERING

37. WEE WILLIE WINKIE. The author is little-remembered William Miller.

38. WHIP. The first whip was Congressman James Watson, a Republican, in 1899.

39. WEIMARANER

40. *WE*, a book published in 1927. Lindbergh won a Pulitzer Prize for his autobiography, *The Spirit of St. Louis*, in 1953.

41. WEASEL WORD

42. The WAILING WALL. It is part of an ancient temple destroyed in 70 A.D. by the Romans.

43. WELTERWEIGHT

44. The WHIFFENPOOFS

45. DR. WATSON

46. WEARY WILLIE

47. WALTER WINCHELL

48. WALTZING. Waltzing Matilda refers to traveling on foot (waltzing) and carrying a pack (Matilda).

49. The WINDPIPE

50. WHO, WHAT, WHEN, WHERE, WHY. Along with How, they constitute the six points to incorporate in a piece of writing. See epigraph of B section.

Y Z Answers

1. YOGA, becoming more and more popular in the West.
2. ZEBU
3. YIDDISH
4. ZUCCHINI
5. YIN AND YANG. *Yin* is dark, female, negative, and *yang* is light, male, and positive. Harmony is achieved when the two forces are balanced.
6. YUPPIES
7. YOSEMITE. It has spectacular canyons and mountains.
8. YARBOROUGH, named after Charles Worsley, 2nd Earl of Yarborough.
9. ZOOT SUIT
10. ZILLION
11. YUCCA
12. ZINNIA
13. YANGTZE
14. ZODIAC. Each division is named after a constellation: Aries, Taurus, Gemini, Cancer, Leo, Virgo, Libra, Scorpio, Sagittarius, Capricorn, Aquarius, Pisces.
15. YARMULKE
16. ZEUS
17. ZEITGEIST
18. ZONE, as in Zone Improvement Plan.
19. YALTA
20. YEAR
21. ZEISS, Carl
22. YAM
23. ZAHARIAS, "Babe" (Mildred) Didrickson

24. YES-MAN
25. ZED
26. YO-YO
27. YEOMAN
28. YOGURT
29. ZOMBIE
30. ZOYSIA
31. YAK. Domesticated yaks serve as draft animals and are used for meat and milk.
32. *ZELIG*
33. ZUIDER ZEE
34. *The YEARLING*
35. ZITHER
36. YALE, Elihu. He donated a large sum to The Collegiate School at New Haven, Connecticut. The school was later renamed Yale University.
37. The YAHOOS
38. ZEBRA
39. ZIRCON
40. YORICK, jester to the King of Denmark in *Hamlet*.
41. YEN
42. YELLOWSTONE, home of the "Old Faithful" geyser.
43. ZEPPELIN. Von Zeppelin was a German general who experimented with dirigible balloons and invented the first rigid airship in 1900. Germany used some of his ships in World War I.
44. YELLOW JACKET
45. YAOUNDÉ
46. YERKES. Financed by Charles Yerkes, this observatory of the University of Chicago is located in Wisconsin.
47. ZYGOTE
48. YEW
49. ZENITH
50. ZUNI. Many of this tribe live in New Mexico.

Answers to
Section II

Political Parties

1. States Rights Democrat
2. Anti-Masonic
3. Constitution-Union
4. Socialist
5. Anti-Federalist
6. American
7. Democrat
8. Whig
9. Greenback
10. Independent
11. Republican
12. Prohibition
13. Progressive
14. Union
15. Federalist

Foreign Words

1. physician
2. frog
3. war
4. pig
5. money
6. finger
7. butterfly
8. love
9. soup
10. tomato
11. zero
12. tooth
13. tall
14. sugar
15. minute

Astronomy

1. moon
2. Copernicus
3. The Big Dipper
4. earth
5. Jupiter
6. universe
7. the calendar
8. time
9. galaxies
10. asteroids
11. ozone layer or ozone shield
12. neutron star

Literary Characters

1. *Oliver Twist* by Dickens
2. *The Sketch Book* by Washington Irving
3. Esmerelda
4. Christian
5. Sancho Panza
6. Rabelais
7. Elaine
8. Rebecca (Becky) Sharp
9. Charlotte Brontë
10. Kim (Kimball O'Hara)
11. Hypatia
12. *Les Miserables* by Victor Hugo

Mythology

1. Atlas
2. Eos
3. Pegasus
4. Sisyphus
5. Calliope
6. Pan
7. Styx
8. Echo
9. Adonis
10. Janus
11. Endymion
12. hippogriff

Anatomy

1. cranium
2. diaphragm
3. alimentary canal
4. nostrils
5. lymph
6. sclera
7. skin
8. lunula
9. deltoid
10. the foot
11. ligaments
12. aorta

The Dance

1. mazurka
2. hula
3. tarantella
4. tango
5. schottische
6. Charleston
7. minuet
8. shimmy
9. beguine
10. adagio
11. ballet
12. hornpipe

Sea Creatures

 1. sea horse
 2. whale
 3. dugong
 4. walrus
 5. oyster
 6. shark
 7. Portuguese man-of-war
 8. sea turtle
 9. otter
10. sardine
11. sponge
12. ocean perch

Art

1. Winslow Homer
2. Grandma Moses (Anna Mary Robertson Moses)
3. bas relief
4. Paul Klee
5. *The Age of Innocence*
6. *Aurora*
7. trompe l'oeil
8. *The Last Supper*
9. Andy Warhol
10. Gilbert Stuart
11. Rembrandt
12. James E. Fraser

Music

1. Johann Strauss
2. Nicolay Rimsky-Korsakov, in his opera *Sadko*.
3. percussion
4. George Frideric Handel
5. Franz Liszt
6. Stephen Collins Foster
7. breve
8. aria
9. saxophone
10. New York Philharmonic
11. serenade
12. coda

Architecture

1. Knossos, on the island of Crete.
2. Chartres Cathedral
3. Frank Lloyd Wright
4. Buckminster Fuller
5. Trans World Airlines Terminal
6. apse
7. Sir Christopher Wren
8. the Egyptian pyramids
9. the Pantheon
10. the Cloisters
11. James Russell Lowell
12. Walter Gropius

Countries of the World

1. Bangladesh
2. Zaire
3. Switzerland
4. Saudi Arabia
5. Australia
6. France
7. Spain
8. Israel
9. Luxembourg
10. Qatar
11. Peru
12. Finland